13/5/12.

# Holding Fast to God

## A REPLY TO DON CUPITT

*Keith Ward*

*Foreword by Sir Norman Anderson*

D1347199

First published 1982
SPCK
Holy Trinity Church
Marylebone Road
London NW1 4DU

Copyright © Keith Ward 1982

British Library Cataloguing in Publication Data

Ward, Keith
    Holding fast to God.
    1. Theology, Doctrinal
    I. Title
    230        BT77.3

    ISBN 0-281-04022-2


Filmset by Pioneer, East Sussex
Printed in Great Britain by
The Anchor Press, Tiptree, Essex

# CONTENTS

# FOREWORD

Keith Ward has done me the honour to ask me to read in draft this 'Reply to Don Cupitt' and to write a Foreword. This I gladly do. I have read his manuscript with much interest and profit.

It is easy enough to counter Cupitt's arguments by a 'confessio fidei', as I did myself recently at a meeting of an undergraduate society. He had been asked to speak on 'God without myth'; but what he said would, I think, have been better entitled 'Symbol without substance'. But the trouble about such a discussion is that Cupitt is apt to dogmatize (in the nicest possible way) about the things he asserts that no intelligent person could possibly believe today; so two diametrically different points of view are put forward, without any real meeting of minds. But this positive dialogue is precisely what Keith Ward is admirably qualified to promote.

He was himself already teaching philosophy in British universities when he moved from a position of complete atheism to what he describes as 'a fairly traditional Christian view'. He believes (rightly, as I see it) that Cupitt's curious blend of Logical Positivist philosophy, scientific theory and quasi-Buddhist agnosticism simply 'will not do'. The God from whom Cupitt was 'taking leave' in 1980 is emphatically *not* the God whom Jesus revealed and whom Christians worship. So in place of Cupitt's insistence on modern man's 'autonomy' (a word which he uses, in Ward's analysis, in at least eight different senses!) from an arbitrary despot before whom it would be 'odious to grovel', Ward writes of a supremely loving Creator and asks: 'To obey that God, to receive from his hand what he is pleased to give, to be raised up by him to share in his life; what more could one ask?'

This is a book I could never have written myself, for I am no philosopher; and there are a few statements I should wish to express somewhat differently. But I greatly admire the frankness and remorseless logic with which Keith Ward deals with point after point, and I deeply appreciate the way in which he continually comes back to the 'forgiveness, reconciliation and redemption' made freely available at the cross (as 'an offering, not of the death of a man, but of the life of God') and to the paradigmatic, historical miracle of the resurrection (which he spells out in considerable detail). To him the Christian concept of God is always 'of a God who becomes man, who suffers and dies;

who expresses his being for ever in the form of the risen and glorified Christ; and who transforms our personalities from within, by our free and co-operative consent, into the image and likeness of Christ'.

*Cambridge*                                           NORMAN ANDERSON
*May 1982*

# INTRODUCTION

Is Christianity credible today? Can we any longer believe in an objectively existing, perfect God, who has created the universe for a purpose, and acts to achieve that purpose in particular historical events? Well, of course, many highly intelligent people do. And yet it may be felt that there are reasons why they should not, if they really took account of the vast change in human knowledge that has come about since the rise of the sciences. Maybe the scientific world-outlook is incompatible with traditional religion, and the whole thing needs rethinking.

Don Cupitt, Dean of Emmanuel College, Cambridge, is a priest of the Church of England who speaks for those who feel that this is so. Of course there have been many unbelievers and atheists who have attacked the Church; we are used to living with that. But there have not been so many from inside the Church itself, who have spoken out for a radical rethinking of faith. Though some would think it sheer perversity or even treachery for a priest to criticize his own tradition so radically, others have felt it as a breath of honesty and fresh air. Many people who have felt uneasy at the traditional view of God as the all-watching super-person, interfering to cause rain or drought or to answer prayers (if this is the traditional view) have read Cupitt with a sigh of relief. He is prepared to bring the problems into the open; to refuse to hide behind dogma; to search for the real root of religious faith, in a commitment to a way of life which is both demanding and liberating.

There are, I think, four main reasons why people rightly feel uneasy with much conventional religious thought. First, the amazing growth of the sciences has completely changed our general view of the world. We now know, with a high degree of assurance, where we are in the universe — and it is a long way from the centre. We know the basic laws of physics; we can control our lives to a very great degree; we accept that the world is a continuous natural process, developing in accordance with simple laws, discoverable by human reason. That is a truth. It naturally requires us to modify all pre-scientific views of the nature of the world, including those found in or implied by the Bible. It requires us to accept the primacy of scientific method as a way of discovering truth. So it seems that religious beliefs must adapt to the scientific world-view. But how many changes might this require? Rejection of a six-thousand-year time span for creation? Rejection of a God just above the clouds? Rejection of

Divine interferences in nature? Rejection of belief in bad and good spirits, demons and angels? Where will it stop? How much of traditional faith must go? This is the first main problem of modern religious thought, and Cupitt's solution is characteristically bold. He suggests that all the allegedly fact-stating, pre-scientific beliefs must go, and make way for pure science. Only the sciences can tell us the facts; faith must withdraw from any vain attempt to provide truths about how the world really is.

A second main problem is brought about by the application of critical thinking, in history, literature, sociology and psychology, to the documents of the Bible. We can no longer regard them as having descended from heaven, untouched by human reflection. We must see them as historical documents, bearing the imprint of their times, with accretions of legend, moralization and polemic abounding. So the problem comes in the form, 'How much of the Bible can I believe any more, if it is not literally dictated truth from God himself?' How can we know what Jesus was really like, or what he really said, from documents so fragmentary, ancient and obscure? Again, Cupitt faces the issue squarely and goes for the bold surgical stroke — the Christ of faith must be severed from the virtually unknown Jesus of history. Christian faith must be freed from dependence on always uncertain historical research and debate. Such stories from the past can only be accepted as stories, largely fictions no doubt, to help us live the truly spiritual life. Religion, says Cupitt, is not really about ancient history, any more than it is about ancient science. It is about an inner spiritual growth towards disinterested love, and we must not entangle that with the ambiguities of history.

A third factor of conventional religion is the way in which the gospel of new life has been almost lost in conservative institutional religion. There, knowledge is used as a tool of power and control. Religion is an oppressive social force, and the idea of God is used to reinforce conventional morality and the social status quo. Marx and Freud, whatever else they have done, have revealed the way in which religion is used as a power of social dominance and psychological repression. Once we learn their message, we can reject authoritarian, heteronomous religion, and grow towards an autonomous, freely chosen and self-created faith. The real message of religion, says Cupitt, is to be free from social and psychological slavery, and become personally creative, self-aware and unafraid to face reality as it is. Faith must be a matter of freedom, not of dogmatic control from outside.

Fourthly, there is a range of philosophical problems which

have become much more acute in recent years. Does it really make sense to talk about survival after death, without a body, or in some other space and time? How could I be the same person without a body? Is the very idea of an infinite, unchanging cosmic mind incoherent? How can God be both timeless and answer prayer and act in history? Does the idea of a perfect being not simply reflect our own ideals, projected on to the universe at large? And how is the existence of an allegedly good God to be reconciled with the vast amount of evil and suffering in the world? These are not new problems, of course. But the precision and clarity which are required in modern philosophy make them especially difficult to answer. And it does seem to be clearer that the traditional arguments for God do not work; and that any talk of disembodied minds collapses into meaninglessness. Modern philosophy is very concerned with meaning and the limits of meaning. It seems that much religious talk, at least when interpreted factually, goes beyond the limits of meaningfulness.

It may seem that religious talk must simply be given up. But Cupitt's answer is more subtle, and owes much, ultimately, to the thought of Wittgenstein. Religious language should be kept, he says, but not interpreted as factual — that is the traditional mistake. Instead, it functions expressively or regulatively. It outlines a way of life, and provides symbols and pictures which enable that way to be followed. Again, what is important is the intrinsic importance of the way itself. It needs no further, outside justification. It cannot be proved by reason or science. It is intrinsically worth while; and we must freely choose it for that reason alone. Cupitt's message is: do not confuse religion with metaphysics; and there is no need to found religion on metaphysics, either. Let it be what it is, a way of living, of growing creatively, outlined by distinctive and irreducible symbols and rituals.

It can be seen how Cupitt is recommending a bold but basically simple response to the problems facing religious belief today. There are great intellectual problems facing anyone who tries to interpret religious belief realistically or factually. Those problems can be eradicated if one withdraws the factual claim, whether in metaphysics, science, history or psychology, and stresses the life of religion as something distinctive and important in its own right. Moreover, faith should not always be faced with critical doubt, and forced to relapse into dogmatism. It is better to face up to all criticisms, in the assurance that what one has left is of such value that it cannot be dissolved away. Religion is about moral commitment, about a way of living. The old interpretations, says Cupitt, are both intellectually bankrupt and morally objectionable. Religion can live and thrive again when it comes to its true self, and stops pretending to be something else.

What Cupitt has done is to identify clearly and bring out into the open the main problems confronting the believer today. He voices the inner doubts and hesitations of many believers, and forces them to greater honesty and clarity. He is a theological gadfly, driving us to ask again the central question, 'What is faith really and primarily about? What must be changed, in the light of modern knowledge?' For that, we owe him an immense debt, even in the midst of the discomfort he brings upon us. I hope that this book testifies to that debt, and that it is in no way taken as a condemnation of the difficult way Cupitt has chosen. Yet it has to be said that this is an attack upon all the views he puts forward. For Cupitt is also a dogmatist; and his own dogmas are, in my opinion, both too dogmatic and also wrong. I agree that he has exposed the main problems, and that they are real problems. But I do not agree at all that 'the modern mind' is compelled to accept the radical solution he offers. His diagnosis is right; but his proposed cure for pain is to kill the patient. That does stop the pain; but it also stops the patient. In my view, we have to be prepared to live with the problems to a much greater degree. My reason for writing this reply to his *Taking Leave of God* is to show that there are other options open to the contemporary Christian; and to show that Cupitt's own solution is not in fact very compelling.

I say this with feeling since, in 1972, I wrote a book called *The Concept of God* which was very much influenced by the sorts of views Cupitt holds (though even then, it was not at all so resolutely non-descriptivist). In the ten years since then, I have come to believe in the necessity for a much more positive account of the nature of God, which will be true to a mature Christian faith. My present view is to be found in *Rational Theology and the Creativity of God* (1982), but the arguments there are complicated and rather technical. In this book I have tried to give a more readable account of the matter. In other words, my attack upon Cupitt is also an attack upon a clearer and more uncompromising version of my former self. Any asperity in tone is due to this fact. I hope to show that he is completely wrong; but I believe that it is more important to face for oneself the issues which he raises, and come to one's own conclusions. In that respect at least, we both commend autonomy and fully critical thinking.

# 1

# God and Revelation

'An objective metaphysical God is no longer either intellectually secure nor even morally satisfactory as a basis for the spiritual life.' This statement sets the tone and direction of *Taking Leave of God*, and of Don Cupitt's approach to spirituality. He wants to commend a spirituality, a religious way of life, which does not depend upon belief in such a God. He thinks that the intellectual reasons for believing in such a God are inadequate. Indeed, the very spelling out of the idea of such a God is incoherent. Perhaps worst of all, the existence of such a God would undermine morality and a mature spiritual outlook. Is he right? This is the question with which this book is concerned. I can say with forthright conviction that I believe he is quite wrong on every count. For I think that an adequate spirituality is only fully possible insofar as belief in an objective metaphysical God is affirmed, and that any attempt to combine a Christian with a Buddhist way of life, of the sort C (= Cupitt, and so throughout) suggests, is to attempt a combination of quite incompatible things.

I also think that belief in such a God is not at all out of date or intellectually disreputable. In fact, it is more intellectually defensible and morally necessary now than may have seemed possible, at least among English-speaking philosophers, forty years or so ago. As I see it, C's views have been outdated by rapid advances in philosophy and the natural sciences, and I shall be doing my best to show why this is the case, and how a form of metaphysical theism is much the most reasonable option, in the light of contemporary knowledge of the world. I shall consider C's arguments carefully and in some detail, for they have something important to teach, even though I cannot accept the conclusions he makes from them. He draws attention, in a valuable way, to various mistaken interpretations of belief in God. What he does not see, in my opinion, is that there are other interpretations which can help us to see God in a new and vital light, and which can make theism a compelling and attractive philosophy for the most modern and critical of human beings.

The first question to ask is, 'What is an objective metaphysical God?' A thing exists 'objectively' if it would have certain properties, whether any human being knew about it, believed in it, or not. God is a thing which would exist even if no humans existed at all; so he is objective. The word 'metaphysical' is more difficult, as it has many different meanings in the history of philosophy. I think that C uses it in two main senses. First, 'metaphysics' would give a list of the sorts of things which exist—God would certainly occur in such a list, and he would be a unique sort of thing; he is neither a physical object, nor a number, nor a property, not like anything else at all.

Some people would say that God is not a thing at all; but this is perhaps because they think that the only real things are finite physical objects in space and time. God is not a thing of that sort; but he is, logically, a thing: that is, he can be referred to, identified and can possess various properties. He can, it is true, only be identified by description; but he can be uniquely picked out in that way quite easily. He can be identified uniquely as the one and only creator of everything other than himself and he possesses such properties as knowledge, power and goodness. So he is a 'thing', in the sense of being a logically identifiable possessor of properties.

This leads to the second meaning of 'metaphysical'. In this sense, something is metaphysical if it is 'beyond the physical', that is if it is not locatable in space, and therefore not subject to direct verification or falsification by human sense-organs. God is certainly metaphysical or supernatural in this sense, too. He is the creator of time and space, and so beyond both. Obviously, then, he could not be verified as an object in space. So how do we know if he exists at all? There seem to be three possible ways. First, we could tell that he existed by considering certain general features of the universe or of our ways of thinking about it. Here, the so-called 'proofs of God' come in. Secondly, we could know of him by revelation. Thirdly, it may be possible to have some sort of personal experience of him.

It is possible to think of reason, revelation and experience as three quite distinct sources of knowledge. Experience would consist of certain inner feelings which give a direct knowledge of

God; reason would produce inferential arguments to a First Cause from the observed universe, and revelation would declare a set of propositions, not verifiable by experience or inferable by reason, on the basis of some authority. The three faculties are quite distinct; each is separable from the others and has its proper role. None contradicts the others, but neither does any usurp or threaten or blend integrally with the others.

This view is, I think, artificially neat and very misleading. There can be no experience without some reasoning; no reason without some experiences to work on; no revelation without a good deal of both. 'Revelation' is a personal unveiling of the true nature of reality—its inner character, its purpose and the values and demands it sets before creatures. Like any personal communication, it may be misunderstood and variously interpreted; and it is always apprehended within a particular cultural context and tradition. In other words, what we have is always 'interpreted revelation'. Just as we need to learn to understand what other people say to us—especially people from a very different culture—so we need to learn to understand what God reveals of himself. Revelation is an objective disclosure of something real, but it is always experienced in a particular context and interpreted by a particular mind. Revelation, experience and reason go together.

I reject totally, as C would, the view that revelation consists of a set of propositions somehow dictated inerrantly to passive human transcribers. That seems to be a primitive, magical view which belongs to an age which gave much higher reverence to the written word than we can, and it makes revelation very impersonal and non-historical in an unrealistic way. If we look at the Bible carefully, we will see that revelation is much more complicated, and passes through many different stages. At every stage, it needs to be formulated by human imaginations, responding to insights, inspirations or moments of illumination very hard to put into words.

If we look at the Old Testament, we can see traces of many old tribal stories, inserted to explain various customs or traditions. There are many bits of saga and history, which must have been passed on in oral tradition for many years. There are poems and stories, wise sayings and the treasured utterances of prophets and teachers of old. There are laws, coming from different stages in the history of Israel (some of them refer to a nomadic society, and some to a more settled, agricultural society, for instance); and there is presupposed throughout a background of religious practices about which we now know very little. We have to guess at the rituals and festivals and customs which they take for granted.

Where does revelation come in here? It seems silly to say that only these poems and stories and proverbs were dictated by God, while all the others, which have been lost for ever, were mere human inventions. It is much more sensible to see revelation as the constant pressure, in the history of the Israelites, to raise their minds to a view of God as the morally demanding, providential ruler of the world. This God has, indeed, a special vocation for Israel; but we can see how this calling is continually misunderstood or even rejected. Sometimes God seems to be just a war-god, who will win victories, or a plague-god, who will destroy the wicked, but such primitive views are carefully denied in Job and the later Prophets.

The poets and prophets, priests, historians and story-tellers of Israel gradually built up whole traditions of oral material. Then a series of editors collected them and formed them into what we know today as the books of the Bible. Finally, some committee decided that certain books would be accepted as authoritative for the community, while others were rejected as too fanciful or morally primitive. There was simply no place for passive dictation. What we have is a whole series of people looking prayerfully to God; reflecting on the oral and written traditions that have come down to them, 'collecting and editing', and finally trying to make them into a record of a long series of interactions between God and the Israelites. It is a complex, growing process. So it seems best to say that revelation is not quite separate from reason and experience. It is the pressure of God's objective being, demand and purpose upon the experiences, history and reflections of generations of Israelites.

Obviously, I do not mean to restrict revelation to the Old Testament, but there, in those books, God is gradually making himself known, through poems, stories, histories, laws and sharp experiences of moral calling and judgement, as one who calls Israel to a special vocation in the history of the world. At first, it seemed to many that their vocation was to rule the world in a vast theocracy—the Davidic monarchy, vastly expanded—but it later came to be thought that the true vocation was to be a 'kingdom of priests', testifying to God's moral demands and providence and serving the world for his sake.

If you ask, 'How do you know that there is such a God?', it is striking that no philosophical argument for God is developed in the whole of the Bible. The existence of God is taken for granted. It is not seen to be in need of argument. Reasoning and reflection play a very large part in the Bible, even though they are never put in an abstract form. Patriarchs, kings and prophets are constantly wrestling with the question of what God is like, with what exactly he demands and what his purposes really are. The sort of God depicted in the 'suffering servant' songs of Isaiah seems almost a different being from the god who demands blood-vengeance in the 'holiness code'. The difference has come about because of bitter experience and reflection upon it. The Bible constantly reasons about what God is like; but it never seems to ask seriously whether there is any God at all.

This is quite natural. For the theist, God is not an inference, an absentee entity. He is not an object apart from the universe, of which we can only detect faint traces. On the contrary, he is the mind and heart of the universe itself. To believe in God is to believe that at the heart of all reality, of this very reality in which we exist, is Spirit, Consciousness, Value, Reason and Purpose. We are trying not to convince people by sheer logic that there is some extra object, far beyond the limits of the cosmos, but to get them to discern the existence of objective Spirit, *in and through* the things around them. We are seeking to evoke a way of seeing this world, not to assert the abstract existence of some merely theoretical object.

C says, 'the history of the debate does not entitle us to conclude with certainty that God's existence is either provable or unprovable' (32). Here, he is actually kinder to the traditional proofs of God than many philosophers are. They often say that the proofs certainly cannot work. His purpose is only to say that the proofs cannot give sufficient certainty for a total commitment to an objective God. Yet he seems here to share with them the thought that the *natural* view of the world is an atheistic one. God is an extra entity whose existence has to be inferred. The disagreement between theists and atheists is about whether or not there is one additional entity in the world. All agree about all the other entities: chairs, tables, numbers, people and so on.

But is it the function of a proof of God to demonstrate the

existence of an additional entity? And does our commitment depend on the validity of such proofs? Certainly not; the Bible and the vast majority of Christians never bother with them. What bothers them is whether there is a personal depth of reality and whether it has made itself known — revealed itself — in and through the history of Israel; and, if so, what does it require of us? We no more need to prove the existence of God than we need to prove the existence of our friends. Given the fundamental belief that reality expresses Spirit, what we need to know is, where is it best, most fully, expressed?

Does that mean the proofs are a waste of time? No; but they were carefully worked out within a tradition which accepted revelation as final, in the light of the Greek tradition of speculative inquiry into nature. What they aimed to do was to show not that a God existed but that the nature of the spiritual reality which had revealed itself in the biblical tradition was 'God', the self-existent perfect being of Aristotle's philosophy. In other words, the traditional theologians, such as Thomas Aquinas, already took it for granted that God existed and had revealed himself. They wanted to explore the nature of that God and, in particular, to show that it accorded with the best insights of Aristotle, 'the master of all who know'. To demonstrate that 'God' exists is to show that the being which reveals itself in the Bible is none other than the perfect being of Greek thought. It is to spell out theoretically what the world must be like if it is *theios* — God-expressing.

That theoretical spelling-out was a relatively late development and was never received with universal acclaim. Some believers have objected to any attempt to 'prove' the existence of God, whether because they doubted the capacity of reason to discover truths about ultimate reality, or because they thought that a clear proof would undermine the necessity for faith. If God is a basic postulate, then it will be perfectly reasonable to believe in God, even though we cannot find good theoretical reasons for doing so — just as it is reasonable to believe in physical objects or other people's thoughts, even though all the arguments for them we can think of may be bad ones. Since belief in God is not merely a metaphysical theory, but entails a particular way of reacting to all our experiences, the existence of a clear metaphysical proof would be irrelevant to the important question of how we are going to exist and act in the world. We have enough knowledge to enable that practical decision to be made. Further theoretical knowledge might only introduce misleading considerations of prudence, or distract us from the fundamental issue of taking up a living relationship to the personal depth of reality.

I sympathize with these views; a survey of the history of philosophy can easily lead us to be sceptical about the value of any of the many metaphysical systems which litter the intellectual landscape, undisproved but forgotten. To make our belief in the existence of God depend upon such a weak and vacillating faculty as speculative reason seems implausible. Yet, at the same time, we cannot escape the drive to ensure that our beliefs are rational. Something like the traditional proofs must come in, to spell out the rationality of belief, to have a shot at saying what the nature of God is. Our belief may not depend on the proofs; but we need to be assured that our belief is at least rational. If we can find some inconsistency in our belief; if it conflicts with knowledge we have from elsewhere; if it cannot be fitted into some overall view of the universe at all, then it must be modified in some way. It would be rash to claim inconsistency too soon; there is always the possibility of restatement and revision. It would be rash to impose some metaphysical view upon our religious beliefs, when it might be doomed to disappear at any moment. Nevertheless, critical reflection upon belief, using general rational criteria of consistency, coherence, explicability and comprehensiveness, is unavoidable and entirely right.

Such critical reflection has led to major developments in the idea of God, developments which are still in progress. What we now usually call the 'proofs of God' belong to a particular stage in that process of development, when reason of itself was thought to be capable of providing the ultimate truth about the world, at least by some philosophers. But long before that stage, critical reflection was already working upon the natural religious beliefs of the first known human communities.

These early beliefs are very difficult to recover accurately. The days are gone when anthropologists could confidently tell us all about the 'superstitious beliefs' of 'primitive savages'. Now we are at least more aware of the sophistication of early beliefs and of their subtly symbolic, poetic character. But it does appear that in tribal societies, there were usually many spirits and gods, good and evil, wise and stupid, often conceived as quarrelsome superhumans. This idea was soon seen to be inadequate — not because of the rise of science (it did not arise for many centuries), but because of its religious and moral inadequacy. The development of monotheism came in two main forms, the Indian and the Semitic, as the inadequacies of early, unsystematic polytheism were more clearly perceived.

In the Indian tradition, there developed a strong commitment to the ascetic, contemplative life. Through meditation, the sages and *Rishis,* the holy men of India, came to a realization of God as the one, still, blissful, serene centre within the heart. Before this calm silence, the gods faded away as irrelevant, lower-level forces. Perhaps such low spirits existed; or perhaps they were all aspects of the one absolute Brahman. But the realized saint would pass beyond them all to union with the changeless blissful awareness which was within the self. This was not an intellectual process. On the contrary, intellect was often despised as too analytical for the wordless union. It was a claim to experience an apparently boundless, changeless reality beneath the shifting appearances of the finite world. It was seen that the ethnic gods, the gods of a particular culture and society, were largely projections of human interests, needs and values. There was not really one god called Krishna, another called Kali, and so on. There was no way of identifying such gods. The stories about them really served as symbols, expressing the presence of a spiritual reality, which was both in and beyond the events and things of the world, but the true way to that reality was the inner way of meditation and non-attachment.

So it was quite early seen that the ethnic gods were expressions of cultural values, objectifications of human concerns. C is quite right in seeing 'objectification of value' as one main basis of polytheistic belief-systems. At the same time, however, this is not an objectification on to nothing, on to a quite non-spiritual universe. Of course, the way we think of the gods is conditioned by temperament and culture; and it is important to remember this. But people are in these ways trying to formulate imaginative pictures or symbols of real spiritual powers. They do think the ultimate basis of the world is Spirit. Pictures of the gods are ways of seeking to mediate the presence and power of Spirit to particular communities, embracing their own traditions of experience.

The key step is to see that in believing in gods, we are not believing in a lot of superhuman beings, a little more powerful than we are. We are seeking the true nature of reality, insofar as it relates meaningfully to us. We are seeking to relate to the world in its meaning and depth—not just to project onto it our needs; but to find in it a personal or conscious presence. So the Indian sages developed the view that the character of ultimate reality was what they called Brahman—*sat-cit-ananda*—being, consciousness, bliss. This was not just another being which happens to exist, but the real character of all being, hidden beneath a veil of appearances. Brahman is not a person—a finite, temporal object with purposes and needs—but the hidden nature which pervades all reality, yet is beyond all our human categories of description (except that it is spirit, not inert matter).

That is one way to monotheism. It leads to the idea of God not as a finite object in space and time, but as infinite, not really describable; the basis of all finite beings, in them all yet beyond them all, as we see them. God includes all finite things. He is not one of them but is infinite.

This is obviously a philosophical idea. It is an idea which arises in our minds as we think about the world as a whole, and the nature of space, time and finitude. But it did not arise as a result of a bit of abstract thinking in some study. It grew by reflection on a long tradition of the experiences of spiritual teachers, who devoted their lives to knowing the spiritual basis of reality better; and it found its way into the meditations—the Upanishads—which became part of holy Scripture for Hindus. So it is possible to say that it is a revealed, inspired idea, arising in minds guided by God towards knowing him better.

Here is an idea of God as the infinite reality beneath all appearances in space and time. It arose by reasoning about the nature of the world and of the traditional gods; by the experience of great teachers who spent their lives in prayer and meditation; and by the inspired authority of Scripture. Reason, experience and revelation were all involved. None of them infers God from anything. None of them discovers God as an object in the universe. They find God to be the spiritual basis of all reality, which can be discovered by us, hidden deep within our own selves.

There is much that is illuminating and enriching in this idea of an infinite, all-embracing Spirit, of which we are parts. It has an imaginative richness, an emotional depth, as an overall inter-pretation of life, but it raises questions, too. Why did the universe, with all its evil and desire, come to be? Are the old gods with their very personal characteristics, only picturesque baubles for the mob? And what about infinite Spirit itself? How did it come about? Why should it be just the way it is? May it not change out of all recognition? May it not decay and die?

These are abstract, theoretical questions. They were not of much concern in the Indian tradition. Gautama Buddha dismissed them as unsolvable, speculative puzzles and urged his disciples to get on with the practical task of gaining Release, Nirvana. The gurus were too interested in escaping from the world to be very interested in explaining it. Yet we cannot stop such questions arising. They are ways of exploring the limits and effectiveness of our general interpretation of the world. It is an advance of the human spirit to insist on asking them, to seek the best possible explanation and not to be fobbed off by simple appeals to revelation.

It was in Greece that this questioning, analytic power of the human mind was most fully developed. Just as the early Indians were not seriously interested in theoretical inquiry into the world; so the Greeks were not seriously interested in religion. The great philosophers of Greece left the old pantheon of ethnic Greek gods—Zeus, Athene and so on—intact. When they talked, as many of them did, about a great World-Mind or Cosmic Reason, it rarely had religious implications: ordinary people were not usually expected to relate to it, worship it or be seriously affected by it. The questions remained speculative, dispassionate, purely theoretical. The Greeks wondered what the world was really like; but those whose works have come down to us had no great personal concern with salvation or self-transcendence. Even Plato's mystical views manage to make the Supreme Being too much like higher mathematics to seem very appealing. The peculiarity of Greece is that its religious practices never emerged from the ethnic stage. The philosophers analysed and speculated, but there was simply no tradition of growing, developing revelation. So the old gods died with ancient Greek culture. Speculation never connected itself with them. There was no tradition of holy teachers, who could develop the old ways towards a living monotheistic cult; nor were there inspired poets or chroniclers, who could enshrine this process for ever in sacred writings. There were the simple cults and the abstract philosophers. The gulf was too wide. No one could fit the old ways and the new thoughts together.

So Greek religion died in a welter of exotic mystery-cults and occult societies. Some tried to make a religion out of an edited version of Plato's philosophy, but the roots were simply not there. There was no popular piety, no plausible way of making 'the Good' real to people. Religion, it seems, needs to develop from below and within; from mass sentiment and inner needs; from imagination creatively working on ancient myths and archetypes, deep within the unconscious mind. It requires leaders of commitment and charisma; singers and writers of deep imaginative grasp and a transforming vision that comes just at the right time. The time was never right for this Platonic religion. It withered because it was an elegant but pale intellectual plant without emotional depth or moral dynamism. It died; but it was to be strangely reborn within the second great successful movement towards monotheism—the Semitic tradition.

A group of tribes claiming descent from Abraham felt called to be a 'chosen' people, with a special vocation in the world, a special Law and a special destiny (to become a great Kingdom, centred on a Holy City of God's presence). Their tribal god was gradually perceived to be a god who made absolute moral demands and who controlled all human history to accomplish his purposes. So he became the one and only God, with the right to claim total obedience from humanity, the power to bend history to his will and to realize a specific purpose for the human race. There is much less stress on spiritual experience here, but much more stress on morality, historical action and the positive purpose of human life in the world.

Again, it is not fair to view this Semitic god as just a powerful tyrant, issuing moral commands and causing earthquakes when he feels like it. It is slightly odd that C always seems to take such an unfair view of what he calls the 'objective God', but the moral and intellectual inadequacy of such a view was felt centuries ago; it has nothing to do with the objectivity of God. The idea that a powerful tyrant could just tell us what to do is morally inadequate; that would indeed be an infantile morality of slavish obedience. Intellectually, such a God is nowhere to be found; there is no empirical evidence for him or for his punitive or rewarding actions in the world.

The Semitic idea of God never was that he was just one finite being among others, but especially powerful. In talking of God people were talking of the ultimate character of reality, as it related to them. The Israelites felt a quite special sort of relation to this hidden spiritual basis of all beings. They felt that reality was morally demanding. It was not just a set of morally neutral facts. It also and most deeply contained moral demands – not tyrannical demands, but inspiring ideals which claimed their obedience. They felt that there was purpose and direction in the way the world was. This was not an externally imposed and arbitrary purpose, but something intrinsic to reality itself. It was a directed, inner-purposive world, and they felt a particular sense of vocation, of having a task to perform in realizing this purpose; a task which was not self-invented, but given to them by their very existence; a task that was personal, unique and particular.

Obviously, there will be no empirical evidence for the existence of a finite moral tyrant in the universe. The question is rather, whether the universe itself, in its deepest character, is moral and purposive. The facts will not be irrelevant to this question, but, precisely because it is a question about the character of reality as such, ordinary empirical methods will not be adequate to answer it. The question is: does the world express a presence, a moral demand, a purposiveness, which is its deepest character, yet also lies partly hidden beyond the veil of appearances?

It is at this point that the Greek interest in finding a theoretically satisfying explanation of the world returned. The Semitic tradition developed the idea of God, the Eternal, so that people could respond to every aspect of their experience as encounter with a personal, purposive, valuable Spirit, or in times of evil and suffering, as a battle with wills in rebellion against the purposes of such a spirit. God is the mysterious reality, hidden in clouds of darkness, without any visible image, who is nevertheless made known in the challenge of the moral Law, in the great moments of historical redemption from slavery and oppression, and in the promise of the fulness of his presence among his chosen people. He is known in the inspired laws, poems, prophecies and histories which go to form holy Scripture. But the question was bound to arise, how does this God, the God of Abraham, Isaac and Jacob, relate to the other peoples of the world, and, more widely yet, to the whole cosmos? So the Greek interest in the ultimate explanation of the world encounters the desert God, revealed in prophetic fury and the tragic history of Israel. What is the nature of ultimate reality, if it is guided by a being who issues such demands and makes such promises? As he reflects on the idea of God as a personal, valuable and purposing being, the theist quickly begins to detect something unsatisfactory about any idea of a finite, contingent God, an anthropomorphic being who lives just above the clouds and rides upon them like a chariot. He moves on to ask the question, 'Can the universe as a whole be reasonably seen as the expression of personal moral purpose?'

The traditional proofs of God are attempts to show that it is reasonable to see the world in that way. They cannot 'prove' God in the sense that they will convince everybody, however they see the world, that there must be a creator. What they do is to show how the basic way of seeing the world as Spirit, or as expressing a Spiritual reality, fits our experience and our other knowledge. They show how it can make sense of many of our puzzles and feelings. They show what is implicit in interpreting the world in this way. They show that belief in God is both intellectually defensible and morally adequate. But the existence of God can no more be justified than the existence of any other sort of thing—physical objects or persons or space and time. Reason by itself cannot prove the existence of anything. Why should it?

In this first chapter, I have tried to give a brief sketch of how the idea of God developed, in the two great religious traditions, the Indian (Hinduism and Buddhism) and the Semitic (Judaism, Christianity and Islam). In this development, there is a constant appeal to the awareness of the world as an expression of Spirit—especially by saints and religious teachers. There is a reliance on revelation, on the inspired direction of the human mind which discerns the purposes of God in historical events, or which creates holy Scripture. There is also critical reflection on the tradition and the continual attempt to relate it to knowledge of the world as a whole. The objectivity of God, the authority of revelation and the importance of critical reflection do not oppose one another. They need to go together, as the human mind seeks to understand more fully the developing traditions within which God reveals himself.

C seems to think that critical thought is incompatible with the objective existence of God; but that would only be so if revelation was an arbitrary handing down of truths from on high, which human reason could not reflect upon, and if God prohibited all critical thought. Revelation, I have suggested, is the continual pressure of the divine reality upon human minds, raising them to new insights and creative responses. God requires critical thought, as part of that growth into mature personhood which he wills for humankind. So metaphysics — the attempt to relate all our knowledge into one coherent picture of the world — is essential for the person who seeks to respond critically and creatively to his religious tradition; who is concerned to show that his religious beliefs are reasonable and coherent. But belief in God is not founded on metaphysics. It is a basic postulate which expresses a practical commitment, a resolution to *meet* all we experience *as* the manifestation of infinite Spirit, or as the expression of presence, purpose and value. We do not want a merely inferred God. But it is critical, metaphysical reflection, which must attempt to work out a coherent idea of God from our basic religious attitudes and which must attempt to show that the world can be reasonably seen as the expression of personal moral purpose. Reason cannot prove God, but belief in the existence of God should be shown to be reasonable. This is the function of the so-called 'proofs of God', and it is to these that we must now turn.

# 2

# The Proofs of God

It must be admitted that this has been a bad century for God, that is, for the development of a philosophical idea of God. Metaphysics has had a bad name for some years; it has had an uphill battle. It is worth pointing out that this is a rather localized phenomenon. Great metaphysical systems flourish elsewhere in the world: Marxism in Communist societies; philosophical materialism in Australia, Process thought in America, neo-Hegelianism on the European mainland. It is a very myopic view which would take the language-analysis style of English philosophy as the major trend in modern thought. Still, it has undoubtedly been one very influential trend, and it is one which has influenced C quite a lot.

Why has metaphysics come to have a bad name? Largely, I think, because of the attacks made on it by a small group of philosophers (now almost extinct) called Logical Positivists. They were called Positivists, because they held that all genuine knowledge must be confined to the experimental sciences. Any statement, which could not somehow be tested by experiment for its truth or falsity, did not convey any real knowledge. In fact, it was meaningless. They were called Logical, because they tried not just to assert their view as a dogma, but to give it a firm foundation in logic. They invented the Verification Principle, which was meant to be a purely logical principle about the meaning of words. It said (in one of its forms) that the meaning of a statement is its method of verification: that is, if you want to know what a statement means, you have to be able to say what sense-experiences could show it to be true or false. Thus a statement like 'There is a chair outside the door' can be verified by opening the door and having a look. It is therefore meaningful. On the other hand, a statement like, 'God watches over all things', cannot be verified at all. There is no way of showing it to be true or false by any sense-experiences or experiments

15

whatsoever. Therefore, the Logical Positivists said, it is meaningless; it breaks our logical rule for words having meaning.

According to this Verification Principle, all the statements of the experimental sciences naturally turned out to be verifiable, and therefore meaningful. However, nearly all the statements of metaphysics turn out to be meaningless, because there is no way of showing them to be true by experience. If I say that mental substances do not exist, and you say that they do, we cannot rush off to the nearest mental laboratory to check who is right. We will keep on arguing for ever. The same is true about arguments about free-will and determinism, materialism and idealism, theism and atheism. The disputes will go on for ever, since there is no way of settling them. The Positivists therefore adopted the brilliant remedy of declaring all these positions meaningless: not just false, but total gobbledygook. Talk about God is thus quite meaningless, because there is no way of verifying it, and in general, any talk about supernatural entities — ones which we cannot see, touch or feel — will be meaningless, too.

If you believe this, the outlook is not too good for an 'objective metaphysical supernatural God'. Since all such talk is meaningless, we may as well talk about a 'gloobydong tidless gob'; it would make just as much sense. Fortunately, however, the Verification Principle is not a very logical principle after all. Why should we believe that words only have meaning when they refer to objects of sense-experience? There is no rule of logic which says that. Indeed, the principle is virtually self-refuting. For it says that statements which cannot be tested by sense-experience are meaningless. But can it be tested by sense-experience? Of course not; so it is meaningless. Of course, this point was quickly seen; and the Positivists hastened to say that the Verification Principle was not a true statement at all, but just a 'recommendation for the use of words'. Well, if that is all it is, we can decline the recommendation with thanks; and we should also decline the recommendation, if we have any sense, because when you go on to ask what exactly 'verification' is, you get some very odd answers indeed. Some Positivists insisted on 'private verification': that is, we are all supposed to have 'sense-data', and it is the occurrence of one of these that verifies a statement. But most people cannot find their sense-data or do not know what they are. Do you? Isn't talk about such funny things as 'sense-data' just going to get us into one of those irresolvable metaphysical arguments from which the Positivists are trying to escape? Isn't Positivism, Logical or otherwise, in fact a metaphysical system itself, saying that the only real facts are empirical facts, facts we can see, touch or smell? Or, in its more extreme forms, saying that the only real things are sense-data, while physical objects, people and so on are just 'logical constructions' out of sense-data? If that is not a particularly odd metaphysical system, I do not know what is.

There is a very important point here, which is that, if you think hard and clearly enough, you cannot escape having some metaphysical postulate. Even when the Positivists argued that metaphysics was meaningless, they were asserting a metaphysical position, a very restrictive and impoverished one, as it happens. It is just not true that you can avoid metaphysics, at least if you think hard enough. You must have some view, however provisional, of the real nature of things. The theist has his basic postulate, and it is clearly incompatible with the Positivist view. But we are back in the old position that neither of them can disprove the other. It just has to be a matter of assessing the consistency, adequacy and plausibility of the systems as a whole, and seeing which seems to express the truth, as far as one can see.

It is a peculiar irony of C's position that he begins with a protest about subjecting religious truth to a metaphysical dogma (the dogma of objective theism). But he himself has his own straitjacket for religion ready to hand; it is the straitjacket of Positivism. When he says that metaphysics is impossible, he is using it. It is one of the classic self-refutations of philosophy. What is most ironic is that his impassioned plea for the freeing of faith from the shackles of speculative dogma should be stated in terms of one of the oddest dogmas of all time, the dogma of Logical Positivism.

There is, however, a slightly more commonsensical sort of Positivism, which does not talk about sense-data, logical constructions, unified languages of science and private verification. Instead, it claims to represent the plain man's opinion that 'seeing is believing'. It insists that verification is a public thing; that statements should only be accepted as factual if there is some publicly accessible way of checking their truth, of seeing what difference they make. This does sound more acceptable; and it still seems to get rid of the statements about a supernatural God which Positivists do not like. For there is still no way of getting people to agree about God.

The appearance of reasonableness soon disappears, however, when we look at the thing more closely. The claim is that every factual statement must be publicly checkable by informed observers. But suppose that I dream about giraffes tonight. How can anybody else ever check that? After I have woken up, even I cannot check it any more; yet surely it is a factual claim that I did dream about giraffes (not about women). Or suppose I say that I feel very depressed, but I conceal it so well that nobody else knows? Or that I am now thinking about two tons of mashed potatoes — but you will have to take my word for it? There is no way of publicly checking these factual claims; yet they may be very important to me. The Verification Principle is getting less and less plausible.

But there is an even worse objection, one that is finally conclusive. The Verification Principle in fact excludes nothing. For to make it plausible at all, you have to say that statements must be verifiable in principle, not necessarily in fact. For instance, if I say that intelligent beings live on a planet ten or a hundred and ten light-years away, I can certainly never get there to verify my statement. But no one wants to deny that it is a meaningful statement. So we have to say that I could verify it *in principle*. If I could travel faster than light (which is in fact impossible), I could verify it. But now we can no longer put any checks on what possible sorts of experiences there might be, in principle. If I were a fly, I could have a fly's experiences; if I were an angel, I could have an angel's experiences; and if I were God, I could have God's experiences. So now the existence of God, who is an omniscient being, becomes verifiable in principle, since, if I were God, I would be able to check the truth of my own existence and omniscience. It is quite all right to talk about supernatural beings; all we need is supernatural organs of perception. That is not at all what the Positivists wanted. But once they start bringing in that phrase 'in principle', they cannot stop it. This point has in fact provided the basis of a formal logical proof that the Verification Principle cannot exclude anything, by Alonzo Church; but I hope you will take my word for that.

The upshot is that Positivism has only very weak arguments against the meaningfulness of talk about God; so weak, I think, as to be of negligible force. To be fair to C, his position owes more to Immanuel Kant than to recent Positivism. But Kant's own arguments for prohibiting talk about supernatural beings do not fare any better than the Positivists'. He shares with them the view that belief in God must be a matter of argument, of inference and speculative theory; but that is most unlikely to be true. Belief in God is a basic postulate, a direct, non-inferential, practical response to the world as the medium of inter-relation with a personal being of overwhelming value. You cannot be argued into appreciating a work of art or recognizing the claims of another person to your attention and respect. Proofs of God are not speculative inferences; they are directives to a vision of the world as personal, as expressive of Spirit. Of course that entails a metaphysical view, an attempt to achieve a coherent view of the world in the light of this stance and of all our other knowledge, in art, morality and personal relations as well as in the natural sciences. There are so many different areas of knowledge that it is very difficult to get an overall picture, and the pictures of metaphysics will naturally change, as knowledge develops. But they are basically attempts to get an overall vision in the light of all sorts of knowledge—a vision which particular sciences do not try to provide. In this sense, metaphysics is necessary, and the metaphysics of theism is not intrinsically more objectionable than any other. What we have to ask is which view gives a more adequate account of the actual way we see and react to the world and our own existence in it.

If you ask whether we can show such a vision to be finally true, the answer is, I think, yes in principle, but no in practice. We cannot get a person to see the truth of a difficult theory in physics (for example, $E=Mc^2$), without a great deal of special training and years of effort. It is not just a matter of looking and seeing. In the same way, if there is a true view of reality as a whole—and I suppose there must be—we should not expect people to get it just by looking and seeing. There will need to be a vast amount of knowledge, a great deal of intellectual skill, wise judgement and synoptic vision. When we say that there is a God, we are presupposing that the only finally coherent and comprehensive picture of reality is the one in which the whole universe can be seen to flow from a perfect, creative, self-existent reality. That could be established as true by a being of supreme knowledge. But for the foreseeable future, we will have to make do with very inadequate and partial knowledge, very limited sensitivity to many areas of experience, and all the bias with which our own cultural backgrounds and personal temperaments inevitably load us. If there is one true statement about the way the world is, it could be established in principle, but in practice it can never be established, for human beings, because our systems of thought and our range of experience are just not adequate for the job. We cannot establish the truth of an overall picture of the world, but we can still try to get one. However successful we may be in that enterprise, a theist will at least have to say that he is committed to the belief that the world expresses value, purpose and meaning; that is, there must be a metaphysical theory (a theoretical description of the whole of reality) which matches and gives speculative backing to his practical commitment to the world-as-personal: a theory which could in principle be shown to be true. But it does not at all follow that we must now be able to state this theory clearly, or have any idea of how we can in practice begin to convince others of either its truth or its plausibility.

The only real proof of God would be the final elaboration of a theory fully descriptive of the world, within which God had a central and essential place and which explained all other elements of the theory adequately and completely. If so, the best for which we can now hope from arguments for God is that they should offer a reasonable hope of a coherence and explanatory power, which is greater than that of comparable schemes. This, I think, can be achieved. But this discrepancy between principle and practice accounts for the fact that, as C notes, God is said to be both supremely rational and yet also incomprehensible. This sounds paradoxical; C says that it is contradictory. But, given the partiality and finitude of the human mind, it is in fact entirely natural that the supremely rational should be incomprehensible to us. God blinds us, it has been said, not by darkness but by excess of light. He is incomprehensible in the sense that nuclear physics is incomprehensible to a three-year-old. To us, his being is clothed in impenetrable mystery, but in himself he is lucid, self-explanatory, full intelligibility. We are not saying that God cannot be understood at all. On the contrary, Christians do say of God that he really is loving; thus that he knows, acts and feels; he has mental, indeed personal, attributes. But there is much about God that we do not understand; and even those things we do understand to some extent, we do not understand fully. For we are naturally applying words (like 'knowledge' and 'love') to him which we understand as applying to finite things; and presumably they apply to him in a rather different way. It is possible, however, to give fairly clear definitions of these words, as they would apply to a supreme being, without knowing what it is like to be God. Thus, we can say that 'God knows everything', meaning that he entertains all true propositions infallibly, without having the least idea what it would be like to do so.

We start talking about God, when we start adopting a basic reactive attitude to all our experience, an attitude of response to it as expressive of moral purpose. 'God' is that mysterious depth which is mediated in certain symbols and events in our lives; which comes to us as moral challenge, and which can transform us with new vision and power. 'God' is the Boundless, beyond concepts, which is focally expressed in the images built up within religious traditions. That is the root of the theistic attitude; but of course talk of God cannot stop there. The quest for coherence and explanation drives us on to develop a rational explication of this reactive attitude, in its relation to our other knowledge. We then develop a metaphysical theory, within which God becomes a logical individual, an object of reference which can be specified by description.

So we can define and identify God uniquely, in terms of a general theory about the nature of reality. We can apply our terms to him, on the basis of observed facts about the world, as well as on the basis of revelation. We can, for instance, see him as a creative Mind, bringing finite values into being. In the light of this theory, we can interpret many of our experiences as experiences of God, as disclosures of the ultimate ground of explanation and value, which we posit as the basis of our world. The theory provides a metaphysical framework for relating our symbolically expressed responses to the Infinite to our other knowledge and to other human activities.

It is a natural and entirely reputable question to ask what the nature of the world ultimately is. To answer that question, one will need to take into account all available scientific knowledge and also important aspects of human life, such as art, morality, politics and religion. Then one can try to construct a sort of intellectual map of how things seem to us to be, at our present stage of knowledge. It may be that we cannot get a complete picture, because of the very great amount of different knowledge available and the great problems of understanding any of it fully. In that case, we will not get a systematic metaphysics, so much as a set of metaphysical problems and critical queries, put to various branches of particular knowledge. Those who are more confident of systematization will, if they are theists, naturally put 'God' at the apex of their conceptual schemes, as a focal point, a terminus, of explanation and value. Those less optimistic about the possibility of system-building will see the idea of 'God' more as a problematic concept which questions the claims of other sorts of knowledge to be complete; or which probes the limits of our conceptual mapwork.

In either case, metaphysical doctrines of God cannot, in general, be shown to be meaningless or irrational. So there is little reason to deny that language about God is meant to be descriptive and fact-stating. Doctrines about God are attempts to formulate general theories which explain the nature of reality; they are not straightforward empirical assertions, like those about the existence of physical objects. Theistic theories are attempting to relate the basic experience of worship—of life seen as interaction with a supreme objective value—to other knowledge. Thus a metaphysical idea of God is necessary to the religious life, even though it is not the basis of that life, and so does not reduce it to disputable theory.

My own estimate of the present position in English-speaking philosophy is that we have moved out of the phase in which metaphysics was thought to be impossible in principle. It is generally accepted that Logical Positivism was itself a very odd metaphysical view; and it is now scarcely ever maintained in public. The way is open for all sorts of attempts to give an overall view of the state of human knowledge. Materialism, of a rather sophisticated sort, is quite a popular option. Obviously, that is not going to be very helpful for theists; but at least people are not saying that metaphysical talk is gibberish. The way is open for a metaphysical doctrine of God, if we can find a satisfactory one, but there are two main objections to such a doctrine, both of which C mentions. First, he holds that the traditional proofs have broken down, so that there are no good reasons for believing in God; secondly, the concept of God is internally incoherent; it contains contradictions—God's goodness is incompatible with evil; his omnipotence is incompatible with freedom; and he is supposed to be immutable and personal at the same time. Each of these objections must now be dealt with in turn: I think that they can be dealt with, quite adequately. But it is worth saying that any and every philosophical system will have its problems. There is no clear, non-controversial and completely unproblematic theory, whether it is materialistic or theistic, empiricist or rationalist. So the theist should perhaps not get worried too soon about the problems of his position. You must take them seriously, but they will seldom be such as totally to undermine a position. More often, they will call for reformulation. This is just as it should be, since the bases of our fundamental beliefs do not lie in speculative thought, but in our most basic attitudes to life. So what we are really doing here is asking whether those attitudes can be rationally systematized. We assume that they can in the end, but we must often live with problems that we cannot ourselves resolve. We do not have to have all the answers. Indeed, to see the problems should give us a deeper appreciation of the subtlety and profundity of theism, and a suspicion of any over-easy or lucidly clear answers to the ultimate questions of human nature and destiny. On the one hand, C helps us to see this point, by stressing the subsidiary importance of speculative thinking in religion, but on the other, he himself falls into the trap of giving over-simplified answers, by simply brushing away the whole of traditional theism. It would be better, I think, to retain the tradition and wrestle with it, rather than to jettison it because of some exceedingly dubious philosophical arguments.

Have the traditional proofs of God really broken down? It is true that they were framed in terms of Aristotelian physics, and that has been 'utterly destroyed by the scientific revolution of the seventeenth century' (24). Aristotle's physics has in fact been twice replaced, once by Newton and again by Einstein, but this does not mean that we now believe nature is wholly explicable in its own terms, whereas Aristotle thought it had to be scientifically explained by a 'Most Real Being' outside it. On the contrary, the problem of explanation remains the same now as it ever did. Natural science can certainly stop with a few simple, ultimate laws and a first material state, but the question remains, can those laws and that state be explained? Well, not by the natural sciences. But a proper question remains, now as then, 'Can the ultimate laws of the universe be explained, or are they brute facts we just have to accept?' No scientific advance can help us with this question, for the sciences work within particular frameworks of investigation and do not themselves raise ultimate questions about those frameworks. So there is no scientific answer to this question, whether the universe makes sense, in some ultimate way. The question remains the same for us as it was for Aristotle; though, of course, if we try to answer it, we must take the most recent scientific knowledge into account. One important job of the metaphysical idea of God is that it enables us to say that the world ultimately makes sense, that it is completely intelligible.

Suppose there is no God. Then, sooner or later, you are going to have to say that something just exists, and there is no reason for it. You just have to accept it, and that is all. But we still feel like asking, 'How does it come about that anything exists? Why should there be anything at all?' The atheist may well say that there is no answer to this question. But it is ultimately frustrating to be told that things just are the way they are, and there is no explanation to be had. It is very natural to seek for an explanation, if it could possibly be found. After all, we do believe that we will find reasons for why things happen in the world. The success of the sciences is built on this fact. And we could not live even for a day if we did not assume that there were reasons why things happened as they did; we would never be able to tell what was going to happen next. So we assume there are reasons for things. We are only pushing this assumption to its logical conclusion if we ask for the reason why the universe exists.

But what sort of explanation could be found for the sheer fact of existence? Aristotle gave the outline of what must be the right reply. We look for reasons why things exist, because they are not self-explanatory. They could be different; they are caused by other things. We assume that everything that comes into existence in time is caused by something else, which explains why it has the nature it has. Now if everything was caused by something else, there would never be a final explanation of the universe; the chain of causes would go back for ever. It might do so; but if it did, there would obviously be no complete, final explanation.

So if there is going to be a final explanation, there will have to be something which is not caused, which is not even capable of being caused by anything else. It will have to be something which cannot come into existence in time; that is, it will be timeless. And it will have to be something which is self-explanatory, which actually explains itself. That means, if we saw it and understood it fully, we would see that it could not be different; it has to be the way it is. Philosophers call this a 'necessary being'; one that could not possibly be different, and so could not fail to exist.

If we are going to ask the question about the ultimate

explanation of existence, about why anything exists at all, we find that this question could only be answered if there exists a being which is self-explanatory; which is uncaused and timeless; which could not fail to exist. Of course, we cannot really imagine such a being; but we can have the idea of it. The idea seems to be coherent (it is not self-contradictory); and there must be such a being, if the universe is to be ultimately explicable. The so-called 'First Cause' argument is really an attempt to show that only such a being could provide a final explanation of the universe. Of course, we cannot prove that every event must have a cause, or that there cannot be an infinite regress of causes. But if the universe is finally explicable, then there must eventually be one timeless uncaused necessary being, upon which everything in the universe depends for its existence.

It is obvious that this being is very unlike the anthropomorphic tyrant of whom C most often speaks. It is not one of the finite things in time at all. God is not just another being, like all the rest in the universe, but bigger. Things in the universe change, decay, are dependent in many ways on other things, and have no inherent power of existing. But God, and God alone, is changeless, cannot decay, depends on nothing beyond himself, and has an inherent power of exisiting. He is the one and only self-existent being.

C holds that the First Cause argument has been destroyed by science; for nature, he says, is now seen as being self-contained, not in need of some external explanation. But that is misleadingly put and untrue. It is precisely science, which seeks the greatest possible rational explanation for things, which leads to the conjecture of a final explanation for everything. That ultimate conjecture is bound to be beyond the scope of any particular science, but it can be posited, as the presupposition of the intelligibility of the world, and so of the success of science. The success of the sciences is the best argument for theism there is, for it leads us to seek ever-more complete explanations for things. Nature is only self-contained if there is no complete explanation of it. If there is such an explanation, it must lie in a truly self-existent being; and that will certainly not be part of the world we investigate in the sciences.

C also objects that God does not actually explain anything. But, while it is true that *we* cannot get the full explanation, we can see how there could *be* one, how God really could explain everything, even if in a way we can only dimly understand. And

25

that is certainly a very different belief from the belief that there is no final explanation at all. We can even go on to fill in the sort of explanation this is. So far, we have considered one basic puzzling fact about the world; the fact that it exists at all. But there are three other main puzzling features which lead us to elaborate on the idea of God as the self-existent, eternal being. These features have formed the basis of the traditional 'proofs' of God.

The second feature is the fact of order or design in nature. Nature universally obeys elegant, simple and mathematically precise laws; it is ordered in a rational way. That the world seems to be a rational, necessarily structured whole, following universal simple principles, is certainly a puzzling fact about it. It could have just happened by chance. We might say that, out of an infinite number of possible universes, any one of them is just as improbable as all the others. Yet the apparently rational structure of the world continues to perplex us, and I think the root cause is this: if time really progresses from moment to moment, it is vastly improbable that anything at all should even endure across two successive moments, much less that things should endure over long periods of time in predictable and regular ways. It is rather like a coin coming down on the same side every time, when it is flipped. The more things endure, the more nature goes on being regular, and the more unlikely it is that it is all governed by pure chance. We are induced to think that nature is actually made to be regular by a rational being, whose necessary nature ensures its stability over time. So God, the necessary self-existent being, is seen to have a rational character.

C objects to the design argument that it produces no predictions, and so has no real explanatory force. That is, we cannot use God to predict what sorts of design there will be in nature. But this misses the point. This argument does not show what sorts of design there will be; it asserts that there will always be some sort of order and law-likeness in nature; and that this is necessarily the case, since the cause of the world ensures it. Explanations do not all have to predict—for instance, the explanations provided by historians or literary critics do not predict—but they have to make particular things clearer; they have to make sense of them. The postulate of God does make sense of, explain the fact that, the world is rationally ordered by attributing its existence to a necessarily rational self-existent being.

The third puzzling feature that theistic arguments draw attention to is the existence of consciousness. Again, consciousness could be just a chance, purposeless phenomenon that has happened, and has no ultimate significance in the scheme of things. Yet it is consciousness which reveals the beauty, the order, the value of things, which seems to give the world whatever value it has (an unperceived beauty is not of any value). Consciousness results from a very complex process of evolution, creating the central nervous system and the brain which makes consciousness, as we know it, possible. It looks remarkably like a purposeful process aiming at value. Nature not only looks rationally ordered; it seems to be purposive; and its purpose is increasing complexity of awareness. This suggests that the self-existent cause of all is not only rational, but also purposive.

The fourth feature of the world which points to theism is the existence of moral obligation and human freedom. It is a fact that most people feel themselves to be occasionally confronted by moral obligations which they feel they must obey, without hope of reward and even at great cost. But what sort of world is it which contains such demands and obligations? Again, we can always say that obligations are no more than subjective feelings, bred by our parents or society. Or we can say that they are ultimate facts about the world, and there is no further explanation to be given. Both these answers have been given from time to time. But the puzzle remains. The natural 'home' for a moral demand is not an unconscious, pointless, random collection of sub-personal forces, but a universe of reason, purpose and objectively existing ideals. Our obligations, we might say, are the ideals which draw us towards the fulfilment of our purpose as rational beings; and these ideals are necessary and objective principles, rooted in the real nature of things. If our sense of morality is justified and rational, it is natural to say that the world is not only rational and purposive, but also expressive of ideals, which call us to realize them, to some extent, in our lives. The foundation of a rational morality is the belief that the universe as a whole is expressive of a moral purpose, and is rationally structured to that end.

These are not proofs, in the sense of arguments which no one can deny. They are attempts to show how the idea of God, as a self-existent being with a rational moral purpose, can make sense of various puzzling features of our world; how the idea is internally consistent and coherent with other knowledge that we have. C's arguments against them do not really seem very strong. He points out that the proofs are all capable of attack and of rejection by intelligent people. Of course they are. We may think that the world does not make sense in the end; or that it does not seem consistent with having a moral purpose; or that there is no clear experience of this rather abstract metaphysical God. These judgements are bound up with many factors in our own experience and commitments; they cannot be smoothly argued out of existence. The theist needs to take seriously the facts of evil, seeming senselessness and the apparent hiddenness of God. He will think that these things are explicable, or would be, if we understood God's creation properly. But he must accept that rational judgements on these matters will vary. There is no factor that can rationally compel a decision one way or the other; but there are many factors which can make our decision, whichever way it goes, more rational. It does not matter that the 'proofs' can be attacked; what matters is that they can be the foundation of a rational and informed decision about the question of God's existence.

We must be careful not to be dominated by some metaphysical system. Yet metaphysics is essential, so long as it is not the foundation of faith, but the exploration of its presuppositions. Keeping our eyes always upon the knowledge of the living God through Jesus Christ— which is the real foundation of faith— we need to ask, Is our belief reasonable? Does it cohere with contemporary knowledge? So we frame conjectures, hypotheses, which can suggest its rationality. C himself testifies to this very fact when he gives up belief in an objective God largely because he is not convinced by the strength of the traditional arguments. I suggest that the traditional arguments, reformulated for our own day, are more relevant and realistic now than they have seemed for some time. The present state of scientific knowledge is entirely compatible with seeing the world as the expression of the rational moral purpose of a uniquely self-existent being. This is exactly the being which reflective thought about the Semitic tradition of theism leads one to seek, as the basis of faith.

So I do not at all believe that the traditional proofs have broken down, or that 'objective theism' is bound to decline in the modern world. On the contrary, I believe that, after a temporary and superficial rejection of metaphysical thought, reflective people are again looking for an overall view, which will hold together all the different areas of human knowledge and experience in a coherent whole. People see more clearly that a 'proof' is not an infallible argument which will convince all but the stupid. It is a presentation of such an overall view as coherent, adequate, consistent and fruitful in directing our personal attitudes and actions. They see more clearly than C apparently does, that any acceptable view of God will see him as the self-existent One, beyond all finite beings, and not as an interfering busybody, continually fussing about our paltry peccadilloes. Objective theism is in the ascendant; for it is the most coherent and adequate overall view of human existence there is.

One question, however, does remain. Is the self-existent One, of whom I have spoken, really the same God as the Christian God, who acts and loves, becomes man and answers prayers? How can the changeless, timeless and necessary God be quite as active, busy and changing as this? Theism, of a suitably sophisticated sort, may be in the ascendant; but can this really be Christian theism, with its seemingly anthropomorphic personal Father-god? C thinks not; 'The regular cosmic God and the small-scale interventionist, personal God—do not fit well together and never did', he says (105). To this question we must now turn.

# 3

# The Nature of God

What sort of God is it of which C is taking leave? Is it really the God of Christian orthodoxy, or is it an alien monster of his own invention? It is quite revealing to look through his book and note the descriptions that he gives of God. Very early on, he says that 'God is conceived as an infinite, almighty and commanding being quite distinct from the believer, who requires absolute obedience' (xii). There is not really much wrong with that; except that already the emphasis on 'commands' and 'absolute obedience' gives an impression of an authoritarian figure who does not like to be questioned, and the stress on distinctness makes God seem remote and unsympathetic.

On p. 7 he states that 'government by personal rule, however enlightened, is always in the long run morally intolerable and spiritually oppressive'. This obviously applies to God, who is thus again seen as denying human freedom and enforcing absolute conformity to tradition. 'The God of objective monotheism is traditional culture personified' (20), he says. God is an absolute monarch who enforces a static, traditional morality and backs it up with threats and promises. He is 'an alien almighty and commanding will' (85), before which we can only grovel helplessly. It is clear that C cannot think of God as being almighty, without also thinking of God as an alien power, who crushes our individuality by his immoral and arbitrary decrees. He sees no way of reconciling divine omnipotence, human freedom and moral dignity.

It is very strange that he should take this view of God, because he also takes quite a different view, when he says 'God is a unifying symbol that eloquently personifies and represents to us everything that spirituality requires of us' (9). As long as God does not really exist, he is absolutely ideal. He is the ideal to which we are all striving, a being 'energetic, lucid, creative and autonomous', having perfect self-knowledge and self-possession, 'free, sovereign and fully individuated spirit' (108). That is what we all want to be. But none of us can ever be it. If we were, we would be God; and then we would repress all the other people by the mere fact of our existence. C's view seems to be that it would be marvellous to be sovereign and fully individuated; it would be marvellous for us, but terrible for everybody else. So God can only be a (fortunately) impossible ideal, not a real being at all.

I do not think that this view makes much sense. Why could there not be an energetic, creative, sovereign being which at the same time encouraged other beings to be energetic, creative and sovereign? Well, obviously there can only be one absolutely sovereign being; we cannot all be equally powerful. Some of us will have to take a lower place. But it is a bit much to ask for complete and absolute freedom, anyway. Most of us would be well content with a fairly large degree of freedom; large enough to let us have a reasonable chance of getting what we wanted, most of the time. Now why could there not be one sovereign being, who was powerful enough to ensure that we could have this quite large degree of freedom? He could give us the materials to work on, the energy to do the work, and then leave us to it, encouraging and helping when asked to do so.

In other words, should C really find himself forced to opt either for a spiritually ideal being who cannot exist or for an existent almighty God who is bound to be morally oppressive? Surely the spiritually ideal being would be one who could both exist, and not oppress other beings, but give them at least a fair share of freedom. Would not this spiritually ideal being be precisely the God of Christian orthodoxy, who freely creates a universe of free beings, who can aim at, and have a fair chance of getting, a reasonable share of whatever spiritual values there are?

I am sure the answer to this question should be yes. The God whom C cannot abide is not the Christian God, the God revealed in Christ; and the real God is very like C's religious ideal, except that he exists. C's arguments for taking leave of God have missed the point, by simply talking about the wrong God. I hope that we would all take leave of his God, but I hope also that few would be tempted to think that his God was either the traditional Christian God or the God of living Christian experience. The one basic point which seems to underlie all his arguments on this issue is his implicit claim that the Christian idea of God is incompatible with belief in human freedom. But omnipotence and human freedom can and should go together. In fact, only omnipotence can ensure that freedom will be preserved and that the purposes which it serves can be realized.

I want now to show, as briefly as I can, how omnipotence and freedom can go together, but before I can do so, I will need to say something about God's omnipotence. I ended the previous chapter with a dilemma, or an alleged dilemma. It was the dilemma of how an immutable, necessary, self-existent God — the God of rational theology — could be identical with the active, incarnate, redeeming God of the New Testament. When C presents his picture of God, he combines the philosopher's doctrine of omnipotence with the interventionist idea of an interfering personal godlet. So he gets the worst of all possible gods: an interfering busybody with unlimited power. It is essential to get rid of this idea of 'omnipotence' as the possession of ultimate power by a person of dubious moral character. God is omnipotent, because all other things must depend completely upon the power of the one and only self-existent being. Their power will be limited by him and indeed entirely given by him. Thus he will be more powerful than any other being which could possibly exist. But, as we saw in the last chapter, this self-existent being must also be immutable and necessary. He cannot be an arbitrary, changeable or whimsical tyrant. If he is really to be the complete explanation of the world, he must be changeless and necessarily what he is. Not only that. If the world is fully explicable, it must be true that *ex nihilo nihil fit* — nothing comes from nothing. If all things can be explained by reference to the being of God, he must contain in himself the idea of every possible world that could ever exist. He must also contain some principle for selecting one world — this one — to become actual.

This God is very far from being a supreme despot. He is much nearer to the impersonal and absolute reality which is a central part of the Indian tradition. When Brahman — absolute reality — is spoken of as the impersonal self-existent reality of which our world is an appearance in time, we can recognize the omnipotent God of the Christian tradition much better than we can in the picture of an old man with a beard on the ceiling of the Sistine chapel. It is a pity that that picture was ever painted, for the God of traditional Christian theology is certainly the non-anthropomorphic eternal and immutable source of all beings, neither Michelangelo's representation of an old man nor the invisible

Superman of whom C disparagingly speaks.

Yet this cannot be the whole story, for Christians also want to say that God acts freely in creating the world, in redeeming it, in answering prayer and in guiding his creatures when they turn to him. The Christian God is surely, above all, a God who acts, and who acts freely. Moreover, human beings are, or seem to be, morally free; and so there must be real open alternatives in the world. If the world followed necessarily from the being of God, then determinism would be true. Our sense of freedom would be illusory; nothing could ever be other than it is; moral effort and struggle would be a waste of time. So Christians want a God who acts freely, and a world in which creatures act freely, as well. How is this compatible with the existence of God, a changeless being who completely explains everything that happens?

The solution to this difficulty is surprisingly simple. It is that the attributes of God which have been mentioned so far do not give a complete and exhaustive account of God! They tell only half the story. God is necessary and changeless in some respects; but free and changing in others. God is necessary and changeless in his general *nature* but that nature is the nature of a creative, temporal agent, the personal God revealed, so Christians believe, in Christ.

Since God is a free personal agent, he can choose to bring into existence any sort of world he likes, just because it is good or realizes some sorts of value. Remember, however, that God's likes and desires cannot be arbitrary; they are parts of his necessary nature. God necessarily likes what is good, what is truly of value (in fact, the 'valuable' is what could reasonably be chosen by any wise being with total power and knowledge). Some philosophers (notably Leibniz) have thought that, if this is true, God will have to create the best possible world. But there is no such thing. There are so many different sorts of value, which cannot really be compared with one another, that no one world is the best. Just imagine trying to decide who was the most beautiful possible woman, or which was the best possible symphony—the whole idea is absurd. The idea of a best possible world, in all respects, is even more absurd. If there are many good worlds, each of them good in different and unique ways, God is quite free to choose any one of them. Whatever he chooses, must be chosen because of its value; since God is necessarily good, he cannot choose an evil world. But God is free to choose between a possibly infinite set of different valuable worlds.

I have just said that God is necessarily good, but how do I know that is true? Well, we have seen that God must be omnipotent, and that, if the world contains real freedom, it must also contain real alternatives; it cannot follow necessarily from some impersonal, unconscious force or energy. What is necessary can only produce things which are necessary. So, if things in the world are free, their cause — God — must also be free. In other words, the world does not just arise from God by some unconscious and necessary process; it must be freely chosen. It is no accident that in the Indian tradition, morality and historical purpose are not stressed, and religious life is more a matter of withdrawal and meditation, seeking unity with an impersonal Absolute. For in that tradition, the world is not freely chosen; it simply emanates or overflows from God by necessity. Where there is freedom, there must be choice, and where there is choice, there must be knowledge. The choosing being must know what it is choosing between. So the creator of a world of free beings must be omniscient. It must know everything which is possible, so that it knows what it is choosing. Not only must all possible worlds be contained in the being of God, necessarily and exhaustively, but he must know them all completely, so that he can choose between them.

Now any omnipotent and omniscient being will be good; for it will know the value of everything, and it will be able to choose things because of that value. The only sensible reason for choosing anything is that it is worth choosing, that it is valued; and whatever is valued by an omniscient and omnipotent being must be truly good, since God cannot be mistaken or unable to realize any possible value.

So we are to think of God as a being with a necessary nature: he is necessarily omnipotent, omniscient and good. All possible worlds exist timelessly in his mind. But he is also a creative, personal agent, who chooses particular states in a creative, rational way, because of their goodness. The world is explained by reference not only to a necessary, immutable being but also to the creative choice of a divine mind, which works within the limits of eternal necessity. This necessity is not imposed on God from outside; it is the being of God itself, which is necessary. In this way, we can hold together the Indian and Greek ideas of God as necessary and changeless, with the Semitic idea of God as personal, creative and active. What must not be forgotten—which I think C forgets—is that God is not an agent *within* the world. He is not like a person who may keep changing his mind, who is subject to fits of emotion and temperament, who grows old and crotchety, and who can be bribed or flattered or helped in any way by us. Nor is he external to the world, as if he were another limited thing just outside it, but excluded from it for most of the time. God is the personal, creative, directing agency at the heart of the whole universe, changeless and necessary in nature but active and free in the particular acts by which he expresses his nature.

If we can think of God in this way, we avoid C's picture of God as an absolute monarch. For such a monarch is objectionable precisely because he is not necessarily good or rational or wise. If the omnipotent being is necessarily good, changeless in character and absolutely omniscient, however, there could be no possible objection to him on moral grounds. We do not have to oppose 'personal rule' to the rule of law; God unites the best elements of both in himself, by being a loving person who is changelessly reliable and just. Yet it may still be thought that any omnipotent being, however wise and good, would be bound to interfere with human freedom, simply because he takes away the possibility of real decision-making from us. I will briefly try to show how this is a total misunderstanding of omnipotence, and of the Divine nature.

God is certainly omnipotent; he has more power than any other being could possibly have. But once we see that God is a creative agent, and not immutable in every respect, we can interpret omnipotence more realistically as the possession of all powers or potentialities. God is 'potent' for anything; he is capable of creating an infinite number of new things and states. Omnipotence is active and dynamic; it requires temporal, ceaseless change. So, while God is changeless in possessing all possible powers, he constantly changes in the particular way in which he realizes these powers. He is free in the exercise of his unlimited power. So he can, if he wishes, create beings which are free and which he permits to control their own destinies. He could prevent them from doing so at any time, but he can permit them, if he has a higher good in view. In one sense, if God allows us to be free, that limits his power; that is, he will not force us to do things against our wills. But it only limits the *exercise* or use of his power. The power itself remains unlimited; it is restrained only by his choice. So omnipotence and freedom are wholly compatible. God freely chooses to actualize a particular world and then leaves the precise development of that world largely in the hands of creatures. The future is really open and largely under our control. God does not predetermine it, though he could do so, if he wanted. There is an infinite number of possible new experiences and activities, so that creation will never be exhausted. We only see a tiny part of one possible sort of creation. But God is infinitely potential; he is a dynamic power, from which an infinite set of new and different values can always arise. He is not just wholly complete and static, frozen in an eternal completeness. He is dynamic and creative, always moving on to new realizations of his infinite activity. God is the infinite potentiality for good. This is as far as you can get from C's picture of a reactionary, static super-tyrant, always making sure the universe remains the same and conforms to the old unchanging laws.

God is also omniscient; he knows everything any being could ever know. He knows everything that could possibly exist and everything that does actually exist. He knows things, not merely in an abstract, remote sense, but directly and vividly, in the closest possible way. So God is immutable in always responding in the most creative and sensitive way to everything that happens in the world, by the free choices of creatures. But his particular knowledge will naturally change, as creatures in the world act in new and free ways.

No being can know in advance what a truly free agent will choose. He may predict it with very high probability. He may override the agent's freedom, if he wishes. God does both these things in the case of prophecy. Naturally, God foreknows that whatever he will determine, what he has now decided, will be the case, and he has the power to decide to determine as many things as he likes. But if he is free or if he leaves his creatures free, then neither he nor any other being can know in advance exactly what will happen. This is a sort of limit on omniscience; but it is necessary, if there is to be any freedom at all. If no being could possibly know future free acts before they happen, then not even an omniscient being could know them. He just knows everything that any being could possibly know; and surely that is quite enough.

God is supremely blissful. This is because he will obviously choose the highest possible valuable states for himself, and so will be supremely happy. But in the free world, there is much suffering. Now any being which simply ignored this suffering would be less than perfect; it would lack sympathy, which is a great good. If God is supremely good, he must share in the suffering of creatures. This is again a great Christian insight, which the doctrine of atonement and the picture of Christ on the cross make clear. God suffers with and for his creatures, so that he might make them one with him. But how can God be blissful and suffer at the same time? Much traditional Christian thought has been unable to face this question, and has denied that God really suffers— but then, the doctrine of the cross becomes very hard to understand. What we have to say is that God is supremely happy in the contemplation of all those values which he possesses in his own being. He is happy in the contemplation of those values which are being realized in the world. These sorts of happiness are overwhelmingly greater than even the whole sum of the sorrows of the world. Nevertheless, God does share in the sufferings of creatures; and he transmutes these sufferings into forms of happiness which are shaped by them. The sufferings are not just forgotten or swamped by joy; they are used creatively to produce particular forms of experience, which do not just express a self-satisfied pleasure, but rather a complex of feelings which include sorrow, but express overall a deep satisfaction, in seeing that sorrow used, negated and overcome. The happiness of God, we might say, is not the innocent pleasure of a child; it is the deep and unshakable joy of the Christ, who has been crucified but is now glorified and who has transfigured sorrow into a richer apprehension of final well-being. God suffers because of creation; the possibility of the cross exists at the first moment of the world's existence. So his infinite joy is changed by creation; but it cannot be destroyed.

God is supremely wise; knowing all things, knowing what can be done and the best way to do it, he will order all things well. But this wisdom must be restrained by the freedom he gives to creatures to order their own affairs, within limits. God's purposes are altered by human acts; they are thwarted and changed. His wisdom becomes hidden and impossible to pick out clearly, because of the overlapping chains of free creaturely causality. In this respect, God's power is shown in his supreme patience; and his wisdom is shown in his skilful guiding of human wills, which reforges his purpose even as it is destroyed. God's will cannot be finally thwarted; for his will is that we should be free, and that those who would love him, finally will. But his particular purposes for us are continually thwarted, so that the providential guidance of the world is not a clear, developing plan; but appears as a series of hints and prompts and fortuitous coincidences, which enable us to realize our freedom more positively.

We can here see more clearly how the Christian doctrine of the incarnation, which on some views of the world seems so odd and difficult, is in fact entirely natural and comprehensible. It is a natural continuation of the creation, of the divine self-limitation and self-giving which changes even the being of God itself, by relating it truly to creatures. We might see the whole of creation as the incarnation of the eternal being of God in forms of material love; a love given to beings which have a real, if partial, independence and freedom, but which can be brought into a communal relationship with their creator by their free response. In this way, God himself is changed by his involvement in creation. He realizes new values in himself, by relating himself to creatures which he has drawn from nothing towards his own fulness of being. So the creation has real and ultimate significance. By the incarnation, God both gives his own being a new form of expression and gives to creation an absolute value and dignity. The wisdom of God, in a world of freedom, becomes the hidden drawing-power of the cross, 'foolishness to the Greeks', but the power of God to those who see there the form of God's guiding.

God is good in three main senses. First, he chooses to bring things into existence, to create them, because of their value, their goodness. Secondly, he will obviously choose the greatest actual set of values for himself at any time. So he will be the supremely desirable being, with a value greater than any other which can exist. Thirdly, since he contains the ideas of all possible worlds within himself, he will contain the ideas of all moral values and ideals. He will thus be good, in containing all the values and ideals which we are obliged to pursue. He is the source of our moral obligations, an actually existing moral demand.

Since God is good, he wills only good for his creatures, but in our freedom we choose evil. Part of the evil in our natures is an inevitable consequence of a world in which we develop within a competing evolutionary struggle; it is a condition of freedom. But most of it results from the free evil choices of our ancestors over generations, which have now been built into the very structure of social life and make it almost impossible for us to know what is good or to do it. In this world, God does not interfere to do good despite us. In this respect, the Christian image of God as our father can be misleading; for it can lead us to expect that God will prevent the harmful consequences of human actions, just as a human father would. God does care for us; he does grieve over our sufferings; he does desire to lead us to good. But again, the cost of real freedom is that we should take the consequences, often randomly distributed, of evil acts. God does not will evil; but he wills freedom; and he allows the evil which we choose, as a result of freedom. In this world, then, the goodness of God is not a continually watchful protectiveness. That would be the other side of the coin which C rightly rejects, the tyrant prying interfering busybody God who will not let us alone. God's goodness is seen, rather, as the supreme value and desirability which challenges us to follow it, which draws the world to reflect it, and which shares in our disorder in order to bring us to fulfilment.

The common thread running through all these explorations has been the two-stranded thread of love and freedom. God is love, and freely creates us to share in his love. We are free, and it is by responding to love that we can fulfil our freedom. C quite rightly sees the supreme value of freedom—of what he calls 'autonomy'. But he seems entirely to miss the supreme value of love; of an objective God who loves us, and of our love as a right response to God. That is why he takes leave of an objective God; because he cannot see that God is love, and love leaves us free. I am going on in the next chapters to criticise C's arguments in detail. In these first three chapters I have tried to make a more general response to C's claim that 'it is spiritual vulgarity and immaturity to demand an extra-religious reality of God' (10). I hope that at least I have not produced a view which is too spiritually vulgar or too immature; and perhaps that I have produced a view of God which is spiritually quite polite and reasonably grown-up.

God is neither an old man in the sky with a beard, nor a myth for expressing the ideals we happen to invent for ourselves. God is an individual, an existing being, with an immutable and necessary nature, who possesses the greatest actual set of valuable properties at every time, and who possesses power, knowledge, happiness, wisdom and goodness to a maximal degree. He is the one and only self-existent being, the creator of everything other than himself. He is the free creator of a universe which realizes a unique set of values, in which he shares, by a complete and direct knowledge and a fully responsive guidance towards its fulfilment. This idea is true to the biblical tradition, and unites the best features of the Indian and Semitic traditions. It is given new life by modern views on evolution, the importance of human freedom, the unity of nature and the intelligibility of the universe. It reconciles the paradoxes of omnipotence and freedom, predestination and foreknowledge, love and power, time and eternity. It has quite a lot going for it. I think it would be entirely reasonable to accept it.

Of course, it might still seem like a neat, plausible but rather abstract theory. So let me stress again that most of us believe in God because we believe that we experience him, either through beauty, morality or purpose in the world, or as a personal presence sustaining us within. That is, we interpret many of our experiences in terms of the idea of a perfect self-existent creator. This interpretation needs to be shown to be reasonable in the light of other knowledge; and our experience needs to be corroborated, as it is shaped, by a historical community of wise and good men whose own experiences have built up to form the tradition we inherit. But in the end, it is our own experience of a personal reality in and through the world, a moral challenge, a rational order, a providential guiding, an infinite depth to the everyday, however dim or inconstant it is, that sustains our belief in God. To give up the striving for a fuller experience of that sort and the attempt to clarify and expound it in the most adequate metaphysical terms we can find is, in my view, to give up any interest in Christianity.

# 4

## Autonomy

In the first three chapters, I have defended the idea of God as intellectually reputable and morally acceptable, against some of C's criticisms. Now I intend to move on to the attack. It is quite clear that a major theme in C's thought is the theme of autonomy. 'Modern people increasingly demand autonomy', he begins by saying. And he thinks it is largely because we must now have autonomy, if we are going to be properly up-to-date, that the objective God has to go. But what is autonomy? Is it really new? And does it really preclude belief in God? In this chapter, I intend to examine the idea of 'autonomy', as it is used by C; to suggest that the term is positively misleading; and to show that it cannot do the job C thinks it does. Unfortunately, no precise analysis of the term is provided in C's book. It is used in several different senses, usually to oppose positions which are so caricatured as to be unrecognizable by their proponents. 'Modern consciousness,' he says, 'is now almost completely autonomous' (14). That is very nice to know, but what exactly does it mean?

C begins by interpreting autonomy as 'the power of legislating for oneself'; and this is a meaning the word has in politics. It refers to the ideal of self-government and was used by the Greeks to resist the idea of government by outside powers. Each city-state should make its own laws and not be subject to the laws of wider communities. But in this sense, it is very far from obvious that autonomy is growing in the modern world. Whole continents are ruled by governments who allow their subject states no power of legislating for themselves at all. Still, perhaps Western liberals at least now think that people *ought* to legislate for themselves. But even that is false; it is a recipe for anarchy. There is no society in which everyone can legislate for himself. On the contrary, in a democracy you may find yourself committed to being ruled permanently by people of opposed opinions and even nation-states think it right to give up some of their powers to wider alliances or organizations.

Complete self-government is neither prevalent nor desirable in the modern world or any other. Of course we do not want to be subjected to others against our wills. We do not want to be forced to do things we dislike, but neither can we be free to make our own rules, nor do just what we choose, regardless of others. There must be some compromise, whereby we get some things that we want in return for contributing to socially imposed requirements. What we should be looking for is not just autonomy, but a measure of free choice, plus socially responsible conscious-ness and a shaping of desires in conformity with the needs of the social structure. Such a course is only undesirable, when it is assumed that the social structure is radically unjust or oppressive. But even if it is, our aim should be not the old-fashioned liberal idea of personal atomism — autonomy — but the establishment of a just society, in which personal freedom will be given its forms and limits by the social structure. I do not really know how one could possibly establish what 'modern consciousness' is really like, or who is supposed to have it, but in a world dominated by Marxism and the search for social justice, it seems to me patently absurd to say that nowadays most people think that they should be making up their own rules, oblivious of the needs of society or the views of other people. If they are, they should be discouraged as soon as possible. For no society can flourish when everyone makes up his own rules. In a world as interdependent as this, to ask autonomy, either for individuals or for nation-states, is both mad and myopic.

Surely C does not mean this? It is a pity, then, that he says it. But perhaps he means, not that people should make up all their own laws, but that they should just be *morally* autonomous: they should make up their own moral rules. Whatever the laws and customs by which you agree to live, your own personal moral rules must be made up by you. There are philosophers who would defend this line, but their views are widely attacked and passing out of fashion and have never been very widely held by the philosophically uncorrupted. Do we really make up our moral principles? As though we could have made up quite different ones? As though whatever we say, goes, in morality? At this point, C seems to become totally confused. For he repeatedly speaks of moral or religious values as being 'intrinsically authoritative'. Now he never says what this means, either. But I suppose it means that certain things really are valuable in themselves and can be seen to be so. If anyone does not see it, he must be making a mistake; for the authority, being intrinsic, cannot depend on my opinion about it. If 'intrinsic authority' does mean something like that—and C has no other suggestions to make—then I am not free to make up moral rules at all. All I can do is to accept or reject their authority, which is intrinsic to them. This is a very weak sense of autonomy indeed. It is not the second sense just mentioned, of 'making up or inventing values'. But it is a quite opposed, third, sense, of 'personally recognizing something to be a value', that is coming to believe that something is a value, by reflecting upon it. It is a strange sort of autonomy, which turns out to be the same as intuitionism, that is, the view that I 'intuit', or just see to be true, certain moral truths.

Now C complicates things further by adding a fourth sense to all this. For, he says, 'I must appropriate, internalize' the standards by which I live. I must impose them on myself, decide to live by them, apply them to my conduct. Now this is quite distinct from seeing them to be true. I can recognize something to be a value (sense 3) without deciding to live by it myself (sense 4)—as when I admire great gymnasts, without getting on to the parallel bars every day. Now it is obvious that, in morality, I should live by the principles that I profess (it is equally obvious that I do not always do so). So at this point the demand for autonomy has degenerated into the trivial observation that I should put my moral principles into practice. Who on earth is supposed to be denying that?

Needless to say, C invents somebody—an entirely hypothetical theist who lives a life of 'passive obedience to God and tradition'. This poor creature is supposed never to think about what he is doing; it is never supposed to cross his benighted mind that what he thinks is God's will may be his own imagination or desire; he is supposed to do whatever he is told by some unspecified source, without question. He appears to be totally a product of C's imagination. Certainly he cannot represent any reasonably intelligent Christian. For Christians are supposed to wonder what God's will really is; they are supposed to have to apply it to particular new cases themselves; they are required to follow their own consciences, as a primary duty. C's imaginary person would not be someone who did not put his moral principles into practice. He would be someone who simply had no moral principles, whether invented by him or discerned by him to be true.

43

But now C comes up with a fifth sense of 'autonomy': 'you must', he says, 'work things out for yourself'. That sounds all right, until one sees the strange lengths to which he takes it. 'If I do obey a good God,' he goes on, 'any obedience is only meritorious insofar as . . . I would freely choose to obey (his commands) whether God commanded them or not' (ix). This quite incredible statement says that, even if I knew that a good God commanded something of me and knew it with perfect certainty, I should not do it unless I would have done it anyway, without his commanding it. This is indeed working things out for yourself with a vengeance. You simply take no notice of God's commands, unless you happen to have worked them out already.

The idea that there is something infantile or degrading about obeying the clearly known commands of a good God requires a truly Faustian self-deception, a grossly inflated estimate of one's own status in the universe. 'Obedience is sin', says C. But is obedience to parents, to teachers, to the due process of law, to the president or king, sin? Is it only obedience to God, so much wiser, more powerful, better and knowledgeable than any earthly ruler, which is sin? Just think. If God is, as Christians say, perfectly good, all that he commands must be for the good of his creatures; it cannot be arbitrary, immoral or mistaken. Being omniscient, he may very well command something for our good, which we cannot work out for ourselves with any certainty. Is it not then merely silly to refuse to obey him, to do what will most surely lead to our good, in addition to pleasing the being whom we most love and want to please, on the ground that we haven't worked it out for ourselves? It is rather like a first-year mathematics student refusing to do what his teacher tells him, because he has not yet worked out for himself the Euclidian proofs. The name for such conduct is crass stupidity, not moral enlightenment.

The real difficulty about obeying God lies elsewhere, in quite a different place from the one in which C locates it. There is nothing wrong with obeying a good God, and everything wrong with insisting on working things out for yourself, when what you need is to be taught soundly. The difficulty, very well known to the most traditional Christians, is that of knowing that God really has commanded a certain thing. This difficulty is quite genuine, but has nothing to do with autonomy in any of its many conflicting senses. C typically mentions only the most naive possible view of divine commands—as if we just heard God saying something to us and had to obey. For a Christian, God's commands come in a much more indirect way; through the sublime but complicated and often obscure teachings of Jesus; through the Pauline teaching about the inner rule of the Spirit, replacing the written letter of the Law; through the use of reason, trying to trace the signs of divine purpose in the natural order; through listening to the testimony of the whole fellowship of believers down the ages, the Church. On this perfectly traditional view, there is no unmistakable voice down a heavenly telephone line; there can be no question of a 'passive acceptance of tradition'. If we are to grow into 'the maturity of the sons of God', for which the Bible calls, we must learn to be constantly responsive to the leading of the Spirit, as we reflect on that living Word, to whom the Bible points. There is a real sort of personal creativeness called for, in the Christian life; but it is in response to the Word of God, disclosed in the history of his people and in the Bible.

I think the Christian can be quite certain that God has commanded some things:— for example the general desirability of the ideals laid down in the Sermon on the Mount and the necessity of self-denial and unselfish active love of others. We do not invent such things; we may not have worked them out for ourselves (we may have preferred a more comfortable morality of reasonable self-interest); and the intrinsic authority that they possess lies in the fact that God commands them as the way to the true good of all people. We should obey God, not out of fear of punishment or hope for reward, but just because we love him and so want what he wants, as the one truly rational, wise and good cause of all.

On more particular issues, we must be less certain of what God commands. We need to reflect on the general principles involved in the creation of free rational agents by the God who is the Father of Jesus Christ, and apply them to contemporary cases by hard thinking, with great sensitivity. I can see no justification whatever in C's claim that traditional religion provides a 'thoroughly heteronomous external control-system' (xi). On the contrary, the traditional appeal is to right reason, guided by revelation, reflecting on human nature, and appealing to the conscientious agreement of individuals.

It is perhaps at this point that a sixth sense of 'autonomy' makes its appearance; namely, the moral viewpoint that one must seek for 'freedom from convention or stifling tradition'. Once more, I suppose no one would disagree that we need to escape from *stifling* tradition or *mere* convention. But does that mean that we need to reject all conventions and traditions? C could hardly be a Christian at all, or a member of a Cambridge college, unless he placed a fairly high value on tradition. One can be quite aware that traditions are not rationally based, and yet find in them a perfectly satisfying pattern of life. Far from stifling our personalities, they may enable us to discover inner resources in ourselves, as we appropriate them. Surely the fact is that both unthinking adoption of convention and the insistence on absolute autonomy are pathological states of being human. One needs the reflective reinterpretation of tradition, the preservation of what is good, not the rejection wholesale of the past. Such traditions may well contain things that we could not have thought out for ourselves and carry an authority that our own free decision could not give. This is certainly so with the tradition of Christ's life and teachings, which commands a way of life with absolute authority, an authority to which we assent, because it meets our own highest moral perceptions and yet far transcends them.

A number of things can go wrong in religion, as elsewhere. A church may confuse itself with God, and claim an authority which only God has, or it may teach that God is an oppressive Judge, concerned to prevent pleasure wherever it threatens to appear. But these are terrible perversions of Christian faith; they do not in any way represent traditional teaching. If Christians believe that God reveals himself at all, we must accept the authority of that revelation, and we must always bear in mind that what it shows is the way to eternal life—the ultimate pleasure—not a set of repressive conventions.

There are still more different senses of autonomy floating around undigested in C's book. It would prove wearisome to unravel them all. But there are two more that are worth some consideration, before we pass on to other matters. A seventh sense of 'autonomy' is one that has become fashionable among some latter-day dogmatizers of Wittgenstein's sketchy thoughts on religion. They take the expression 'language-game'—which is indeed to be found in the master's work—and use it in a sense entirely contrary to the whole spirit and method of his philosophy; that is, they invent a neat pigeon-hole, which they call a 'religious language-game', and then insist that it is quite different from, or independent of, or irreducible to, other neighbouring language-games. Nothing could be further from Wittgenstein's own procedure than thus to invent a completely general category and then become bothered about what falls into it or out of it. Here is an excellent case where the exploratory model of the pioneer has been turned into the Procrustean bed of the unseeing disciple. Anyway, what results from this mistake is the view that the religious and moral language-games are autonomous and not justifiable in terms of other language-games. So we cannot justify morality in terms of religion, or of anything else either; it must stand, as far as justification goes, entirely on its own. This would certainly be another reason for refusing to base morality upon God or his commands.

But it is in fact almost impossible to separate out a special moral language-game; such a thing would require a Platonizing definition in terms of essential characteristics, whereas Wittgenstein's own method would rather lead one to look for a complex overlapping of varying sorts of language, with no clear borders to be drawn. But if that is so, moral and religious concepts may have areas of overlap, and at least some moral concepts would be closely enmeshed with some religious concepts. That this is the case can be seen if you consider instances of people who have felt specific vocations to adopt a quite new mode of life. They might say that they believed God 'called' them to do this; that they certainly would not have done it without that belief; and that they take it as an absolute obligation to do it. Here, as in many other cases, moral and religious beliefs dovetail; something becomes a unique and personal obligation, because it is felt to be demanded by a God who is, of course, in general good.

Furthermore, it would be absurd to deny the relevance of fact to morality in general. I must know the facts before I can know what I ought to do; I must know the circumstances and probable consequences of my acts. Even though all values cannot be justified solely in terms of the facts, the existence of some facts would justify the adoption of some moral principles. For example, if it is a fact that I was created for a purpose; if there is an eternal life; if I can be united to God by faith, not solely by moral effort; if these things are true, then some of my values may well be different from those of an atheist, who believes none of these things. If there is a God who is the most valuable, and thus the most desirable, being possible, it will only be reasonable to direct much of my life to trying to know him better. Naturally, many moral principles, connected with basic human conduct, will be shared with humanistic atheists, but some of the obligations I take to be most important — to pray, to seek the fruits of the Spirit, to aim at purity of thought — may seem to him misguided or silly. If, then, some important moral principles depend upon my belief in these facts and if these facts are revealed, I can hardly say that all my moral principles must be autonomous. It may well be that C does not believe in revelation in this sense (indeed, he cannot), but that is another story. The point is that there is nothing wrong with having heteronomous moral principles, as long as they are founded upon what one has good reason to believe is a genuine revelation from God.

Now this plainly requires that one believes that there is a God and that he does reveal certain things. These appear to be factual beliefs, and in default of a very subtle explanation, they are. But there is an eighth sense of 'autonomy', closely related to the seventh, according to which religious language is not descriptive or fact-stating. It has its own distinctive sort of status and does not depend at all on external, objective facts. Thus C repeatedly states that 'the factual is non-religious' (45); so that insofar as the question of God is a question of fact, it is not a matter of religion at all. What is one to say to this?

The issue will be taken up in chapter 7, but C would need to justify the claim that there is such a thing as 'religious language'. Is it the same for all religions? How can we decide what it is, what its limits are? Is the belief that there is a supreme being, who will unite us to himself after death, not a religious belief at all? I see little hope of achieving any success in answering such questions, except, of course, by the completely unilluminating Procrustean technique of selecting what suits you and ignoring the rest. People may be mistaken if they think they will live after death, and if they offer flowers to disembodied spirits; but why should they not be religious? Indeed, the things which most clearly divide the great religions of the world are their differences of belief about facts. Did Jesus die on the cross? Did Elijah ascend into heaven? Do we live again on earth in other bodies? The mere fact that C thinks such things are mythical or legendary — to the horror of the orthodox — does not show they are not religious, when taken in their factual sense.

In fact, what C is doing is to propose a quite new understanding of a certain sort of religious belief, in the guise of analysing the language which believers actually now use. There can be a form of religious belief which involves no factual beliefs, though it will turn out, I think, to be pretty vacuous; but there is no reason at all to think that all religious beliefs are non-factual. Certainly, the alleged analysis of 'religious language', which has, of course, never been carried out or even seriously begun, would be laughed out of court by serious students of particular religions; it wholly misinterprets the thought of Wittgenstein, to whom it pays lip-service, and can give no support to the theory that religion is autonomous, in the sense of being non-factual.

Where do things stand, then, with this much-vaunted principle of 'autonomy'? The answer is, in complete confusion. It is never clearly defined. It is used in at least sixteen different, and often incompatible, senses, of which I have distinguished eight. It is, in short, an over-general slogan for a complicated set of attitudes, which it would be better to analyse carefully, one by one. One can see, in a sloppy sort of way, that it is good to think for oneself, to be free from too many external constraints, to be original and critical in thought. In questioning the overriding importance that C gives to autonomy, I am not at all suggesting that one should not think, be critical or original, or that one should be continually pushed around by others. That is hardly the point. The point is, are there truths about God and about his revelation to which we must assent, if our beliefs are to be correct? In some quite unexplained way, C slides from a criticism of unthinking conformity into the rejection of all objective truths about God and his purposes. He does this by means of his indiscriminate use of the word 'autonomy' in so many different senses. What it is important to see is that a defence of critical reflection in thinking is simply irrelevant to the question of whether there are any objective truths about God. That has to be settled on other grounds. Let us henceforth agree to ignore 'autonomy', wherever it occurs, and ask directly about these other grounds. For it may be precisely by critical reflection that one comes to see that certain assertions about God really are true, whether people like it or not.

# 5

## Obeying God's Commands

Why does C object to 'a god who is conceived of as an infinite, almighty and commanding being . . . who requires absolute obedience'? He seems to have both moral and intellectual objections. The moral objection is that one should not obey the commands of an almighty being, as this is beneath one's dignity in some way. But this objection supposes that God is an arbitrary tyrant who just happens to command this, that or the other at his whim; so that obeying him would be irrational obedience. However, it is part of the definition of the infinite God that he is not arbitrary or whimsical; he is precisely not a finite tyrant. His commands arise necessarily from his nature, which is changeless and perfectly good. So they are, on this theory, universal principles directed to the greatest good of creatures. There can be no moral objection to obeying such principles.

But then, C says, if we know that these are good principles, we do not need God to tell them to us. We have to judge God to be good by our own standards, before we can obey him, so obedience does not really come into it. But this objection supposes that we can work out for ourselves all the principles that are for our greatest good. Certainly, we must first judge God to be good by our highest moral standards. But when we have done so and have also judged him to be wise and all-knowing, he may tell us things that we have not worked out for ourselves.

That is certainly possible. Yet now C may say that it would be better if we did work them out for ourselves and anyway, we cannot be sure that God is really telling us things. Some things, however, are within the province of human reason and others are not. We can work out general moral rules, laws of physics, and even, perhaps, the existence of God. All these things we can work out. But the nature of God and his secret purpose for creation (to unite all things to himself in Christ), that we cannot work out. All the philosophers in the world could never work it out, for the simple reason that it depends on God's own self-disclosive and redemptive action and not on some general theory about the world. Just as we cannot work out another person's character or intentions by pure theory, so we cannot know God's intentions by theorizing. He has to make them clearer to us by actions and inspired interpretations. Now C may object that there is no God who acts in such ways. But that is a different question. The point is that, if there was such a God, who revealed himself in personal, unique ways, it would not be better, but be impossible, for us to work these revelations out for ourselves.

What God tells us is not a set of general moral rules, or a set of arbitrary commands. He shows us himself and guides us towards fuller knowledge of him. If he commands obedience to this way, it is because it is the way of life. On the theistic hypothesis, man is essentially and deeply orientated towards a supreme value outside himself. Only in that value, God, can he find his true being. But its nature and the way to it must be disclosed by a personal, self-disclosive act. If we have good reasons for thinking that there is such a God and that he has initiated such a personal act, not discoverable by pure speculation, then we have good reasons for responding to that objective act by obedience to the way of life which it demands. We follow the way of Christ because we believe him to be the supreme revelatory act of God. There can be no moral objections to such obedience, except those founded on human pride and wilful self-sufficiency.

What then of the intellectual objections? Do they fare any better? The question of the reasonableness of belief in a real God and of the way in which he reveals himself have been treated in chapters 1-3 and will be further examined in chapter 7. But there is one theme which seems to be important to C's case, and that is what he calls 'internalization'. He describes it as 'a mighty historical process by which . . . values are withdrawn from external reality and as it were sucked into the individual subject' (3). Values, he claims, used to be thought of as built into external reality in some way, whereas nowadays (at least in some parts of Cambridge, apparently) they have been sucked into the individual, or are generated from within. 'In the old world meanings and values came down from above, but now they come up from below.'

I cannot decide whether it would be preferable to be able to see the world in such very clear-cut terms, where everything falls neatly in suitable dichotomies. Perhaps it would; but the world is not like that. If I was seriously asked whether values came from above or below, outside or inside, I would not know how to begin to answer. If anything is a vast over-simplification, projected on to a reality quite unsuitable to receive it, this is. The difficulty is not to say whether or not it is right; but what on earth it means. I do think it is possible to get a rough idea (no more than that, because it *is* a rough idea) of what he is getting at; but it would be dangerous to try, since the whole dichotomy is so misleading. Up, down; in, out; objective, subjective; realist, expressivist—out they tumble, the tidy pairs of alternatives, putting an end to the possibility of serious thought about complicated matters.

He does seem to hold, however, that the 'objective', factual, world, does not contain any values or meanings. A correct and adequate description of it would consist, ideally, in a set of dispassionate value-neutral objectively checkable precise propositions about purposeless, mechanistic processes. The world itself has no value, no purposes, no spiritual powers, no beauty or moral challenge or rational elegance. It is just one precise mechanical damn thing after another.

This view has been heard before. It is the voice of Positivism, an over-simplified version of Wittgenstein's early work, the *Tractatus,* for which the world is the totality of facts, and facts can all be exhaustively described in value-free precise object terms. It is a voice not much heard today. C's much-vaunted 'modern man', who is supposed to believe all this, is in fact the Western secular intellectual of the 1930s, a rare and almost extinct breed. It is yet another of C's super-Procrustean beds. The ideal underlying it is the ideal of a precise logical language, which will perfectly correspond to what is the case; a combination of Newtonian physics with mathematical logic, providing the unified language of science. There will not have to be these nasty untidy sciences like psychology, sociology and biology. They can all be reduced to physics, whose formulae describe the whole of reality quite adequately. As for art, music, history, philosophy and ethics; why, they deal only with subjective projections, and are not about reality at all.

One has to be very overawed indeed by Newtonian mechanics to think that the real world consists wholly of the objects encompassed by that rather abstract discipline, and one has to neglect entirely the fact that contemporary mathematical physicists have a view of the world which is much more puzzling, much less assured and much less mechanistically precise than that.

Now, of course, it is true that nuclear physicists are not concerned with purposes or values in their experiments. They select certain mathematically formulable values, like mass, velocity and motion, and study their interactions as far as possible in isolation from any other factors. But why should they deny what they are not investigating, or say that what they deal with is the only real objective world? Of course, they do not say any such thing; it was the Positivist philosophers who said it for them. But there has never been a scrap of scientific evidence for the Positivist claim that all factual propositions could somehow be reduced to statements of physics. On the contrary, more and more scientific disciplines are begun every year; the situation becomes more, not less, complex. The programme of scientific reductionism, never very hopeful, recedes from view year by year.

The world, in which we actually move around and which we perceive in our everyday lives, is replete with values and purposes. We see beautiful trees; we see animals trying to get things; our own purposes conflict with those of others; we are moved by the pain and joy of others. Some things really are valuable—they conduce to human flourishing; and others are really harmful—they bring pain and disability. Some activities are really purposeful—the cat stalking its prey—and others are really not—the planets circling the sun. What is the point of saying that the 'real' world is without value or purpose? It can only be a form of metaphysical dogmatism; the theory that the world which we seem to hear and see and inhabit is illusory, while the only real world is made of purposeless, mechanistic, colourless particles, without value or point. In other words, what C is placing before us is a metaphysical dogmatism, a distinction between appearance and reality, between the 'natural', perceived, world and the supernatural, or allegedly underlying reality, of just the sort about which he complains in the case of theism. It just happens that his favoured supernatural world is one of aimless atoms, whereas the theist's supernatural is a conscious supreme Spirit. But theism is no more supernaturalist, realist or heteronomous than materialism. In fact, nothing is calculated to undermine autonomy more effectively than the belief that one is really composed entirely of pointless mechanistic forces, about which one can do absolutely nothing. The tyrant God, about whom C protests, is replaced by the tyrant necessities of chance and mechanistic nature. Either way the free and responsible person disappears. What is needed is to reject both tyrants and to leave a supreme Spirit who creates humans as free and responsible, who respects their freedom and has the power to protect it, but who can help their faint endeavours towards goodness if they wish him to.

This is a good example of the way in which C erects dichotomies which are both intolerable and quite unrecognizable, when examined. Who is the 'ancient man', who thought that his values were built into external reality, to be passively received? Who is the 'modern man', who thinks that his values are made up by himself, and projected on to a completely neutral world? Perhaps some very extreme philosophers have entertained such theories, both in the ancient and in the modern worlds, but the vast majority of philosophers, both ancient and modern, have recognized that the problems of value, purpose and meaning are very complex. They lie in areas peculiarly difficult to analyse. They are connected with consciousness, but also with the recognition of the facts of the case. They have recognized that it is unbearably crude to say either that values lie just in objective reality, without reference to consciousness; or that they are made up by people, whatever the facts. There is a certain appropriateness of response in acknowledging something as a value; and there is no simple way of characterizing it. Certainly, the theist does not have to think of values as lying around in the external world, waiting to be accepted. If he says that the world has value, he implies that God created it so that it might be valued by creatures and that it is worthy of being so valued. Is C really denying that anything is worth valuing, that we just arbitrarily decide to value things? Is he saying that Belsen and Auschwitz were not worth condemning, that we just happen to dislike them? As we have seen, C, like Bertrand Russell before him, draws back at the brink, and says that there are intrinsic values. Yet, he goes on, they are freely adopted and self-imposed. But he cannot have it both ways. If there are intrinsic values, then some things are intrinsically worth valuing; and that is what has usually been meant by those who might say that values are grounded in the nature of objective reality. C is objecting to a figment of his own imagination, and proposing to replace it with a form of dogmatic metaphysical materialism which has been defended by some philosophers from the time of Democritus, but is now, as always, a minority view among serious philosophers. He is certainly not replacing 'tradition' by 'modernity'.

For the theist, the thing that is most intrinsically worth valuing, the most desirable of all things, is God. Worship is far from being a sycophantic bowing and scraping before an oriental despot. It is the sincere acknowledgement of the worth, value and supreme desirability of God; and it comes naturally to anyone who sees God in all his splendour and glory, with a pure and reverent heart. It is the aim of Christians to see God as he really is, and so to be filled with awe and delight in his being. How can one possibly associate this desire, as C does, with conformism to tradition, so that he can say, 'the God of objective monotheism is traditional culture personified' (20)? This is bound to be quite false, unless traditional culture happens to express in some way the perfections of almighty God, which is most unlikely, though rulers may like to claim it from time to time. Once one sees that God is not the petty all-determining tyrant, but the supremely desirable creator, who enables creatures to be truly free (which aimless atoms can never do), all objections to theological realism fade away. C simply has not seen that it is precisely belief that God is not to be just identified with nature which frees man from the dominance of nature and its forms. It enables one to locate values, not just *in* the world, but beyond it, in God, so that, in that light, the world and its structures are always subject to critical scrutiny.

It is not the internalization of values and purposes that is required; *that* undermines freedom and responsibility by subjecting man to the aimless interplay of atoms. What is required is the transcendentalizing of values—their location beyond the structures of nature and human society; together with the absolute demand that they be realized in the world as far as possible. But that is exactly what theism gives. It is only theism that can make values truly intrinsic without identifying them with nature; can license an absolute demand to realize them; and can promise that they will be realized. God does not undermine intrinsic values but undergirds them, giving them objective reality, authority and realization in the world.

We may expect, however, that an old dichotomy will rear its head again, between the 'traditional' view that values are founded on facts (on the will of God) and the 'modern' view that facts are morally neutral, and values must possess their authority in themselves. Passing over the now familiar fact that these generalizations cannot be substantiated by historical research, there is a serious question as to whether values can derive their authority from God. In assessing this question, we must be careful to state the theistic case fairly. God is not just a very powerful being who happens to be there. He is immutable, eternal, and must exist, if there is any world at all, with just the nature he has. He is the most perfect possible being; and saying this implies that 'perfections', or worthwhile properties, are so by necessity, not by arbitrary decree of God. It follows that one could, in principle, say what states are worthwhile without reference to God; indeed, we define God partly in terms of such states. So we could know what states were worth having and aiming at, whether or not there was a God. It may seem that C's case is won; values cannot depend on God. 'The authority of morality in no way depends upon questions of fact' (67).

But we have to ask whether and to what extent such values are realizable and how seriously we should pursue them. If it is all just a matter of our decision, as C suggests, then we might of course decide anything. But it would seem reasonable to say that we should only pursue values to the extent they seem possible; and we might decide not to pursue them very hard—we might prefer a lazier or pleasanter life to an arduous search for a worthwhile state, even though we agreed that state was worthwhile, in the abstract. So, while knowing what states would be worthwhile, we might very reasonably decide to pursue them only to a limited degree, and not too intensely. They are only ideals, after all; we do not have to live up to our ideals; we do not even have to adopt them, if we prefer a life of self-forgetful hedonism.

Suppose that you think the universe is a purely random set of occurrences; that the human race is doomed to extinction, whether soon or late; that no person has immortality; that there are no purposes in nature, nothing at which the whole process is aimed; that we live for a while and then die, with no one to notice or care what we do with our lives but a few similarly doomed individuals. None of all this, says C, should make any difference at all to our basic commitment to values. The moral demand will retain all the authority it ever had; for that authority does not depend upon facts in any way. Even if you could be quite sure of all these things, you still ought to commit yourself to the pursuit of moral values, with total intensity.

Now suppose that you think the universe was created by an almighty and perfectly good being; that the human race is intended to achieve everlasting bliss; that each of us will live for ever; that the whole of our lives has a point and purpose; that God notices and cares about all that we do and become, for he loves each of us intensely and unalterably. This, too, according to C, should make no difference at all to our moral beliefs. This amazingly different view of the world should make no difference to your conduct at all.

Is it not incredible that such huge disagreements about the facts should produce no difference in conduct? It requires a sort of schizophrenia to believe seriously that your moral commitments should be just the same, whatever your beliefs about the facts. Consider the whole idea of there being moral *demands* at all: commands with unconditional authority over our lives. Does that view even make sense, in the purposeless universe of chance? Does it not seem more plausible to attribute such a thought to over-strict 'potty-training', or some such Freudian mechanism? In that universe, there are no unconditional authorities. Autonomy would indeed reign, for the rational agent; that is, we would decide for ourselves how to live, without paying any attention to these quite heteronomous and clearly mythological 'unconditional demands'.

Of course, I could decide to live a life of heroic self-sacrifice. There would be no particular reason why I should; I would just decide to do so. No course of action is much sillier than any other; they are all ultimately pointless. Or I could, more probably, decide for the pursuit of happiness (primarily my own), and live a moderately unselfish but comfortable and self-satisfied life, if I could. I would indeed have a morality, but a fairly restricted and comfortable one — nothing like C's very extreme 'religious requirement'. Whatever my moral views, it would be silly for me to speak of *unconditional* demands. It would be more sensible for me to speak in terms of desires and preferences. But it is true that I could decide to live in any way I chose; no way would be, in absolute terms, more appropriate or reasonable than any other.

Now jump back into the theistic universe. It becomes silly for me to insist on deciding to live in my own way or in terms of a fairly comfortable set of personal desires. For if I do so, I will only succeed in cutting myself progressively off from God, and so from the possibility of everlasting bliss. God actually does issue a set of unconditionally authoritative demands. So they really are binding on me, whatever I may like to think. Only in such a universe does this idea not only make sense, but become objectively true.

C speaks disparagingly of obedience to God, as a sort of 'odious grovelling' before absolute power, but that is to miss the point completely. Once again, we are faced with a totally false dichotomy. On the one hand, we have a mechanistic universe, where talk of moral demands is at best metaphorical, at worst meaningless. The ontology of the mechanistic world allows no place for these free-floating, mysterious 'demands' made by nobody upon everybody. On the other hand, we have a universe run by a power-mad god, where the moral element disappears, and is replaced by a sheer command, backed by threats of punishment or bribes for obedience. In neither world has morality any special, irreducible place; it has been reduced to something other than itself.

Most traditional theists have wanted to preserve the unique place of morality, not *replace* it by God. Religion is not, after all, the same as morality, nor need it threaten to swallow it up. What religion does is provide a metaphysical backing, a rational basis, for a special view of the uniqueness of morality; to provide a wider context within which the irreducible place of morality will be safeguarded.

Morality is basically concerned with the rules which are to govern our conduct. If we are going to try to find a rational morality, we will have to consider whether any rules are more reasonable than others. Immediately, two points of view begin to diverge. From one point of view, we can consider reason quite impartially; we can consider a whole set of people and ask what rules it would be reasonable for them all to adopt, as if we were an impartial spectator of the social scene. From the other point of view, we start from our own position as a member of a particular society, and ask what rules it is most reasonable for me to adopt, or to persuade my society to adopt, to maximize my desires and purposes. Impartial reason and self-interested reason provide two quite different approaches to the question of morality, even though they will overlap in practice, but, from both points of view, I cannot decide what rules are most reasonable without first finding out what the desires and purposes of the people in question are, and what the chances of realizing them actually are. In general, the rules of impartial reason will be those capable of maximizing most people's desires and purposes. The rules of self-interested reason will be those capable of maximizing my own desires and purposes.

The theist does have something relevant to say about these desires and purposes. First, he will say that some things really are more desirable than others: knowledge is more desirable than ignorance, freedom than constraint, happiness than sorrow. Most importantly, there is one thing more desirable than anything else, and that is God. The most rational desires are those directed to the most desirable things; so the most reasonable desire is to know and share in the life of God, if that is possible. The Christian thinks this is possible, through grace. So we need to take into account this most rational desire of everyone (even though most people may not actually have it); rational moral rules will seek to maximize our chances of realizing it.

Secondly, the theist will say that not only do people have their own particular purposes but God has created everyone for an objective purpose. If my very being is created in order to realize a purpose, it is most reasonable to seek to discover it and make it my own, that is, to conform my life to it. Rational moral rules will seek to conform people most closely to their true, God-given purpose.

If there is a God, it is thus supremely rational to seek to share in his life and conform to his purposes; these are attainable goals, to which all others will be subordinated, if we are reasonable. It can be seen how talk of 'unconditional demands' seems rather alien to this whole way of thought. Such talk belongs more to the philosophy of Kant, who was not a practising Christian at all, than to the tradition of the Church, which has preferred to speak in terms of desires and natural inclinations. It is very odd that C retains such Kantian terminology, when rejecting Kant's own subtle arguments for God. In the main tradition of Christianity, God is not the arbitrary commander; he is the supreme object of desire and the purposive creator. The moral rules, which reason must work out on the basis of these facts, will depend on investigation into the structures of the created order (which may be presumed to express or foreshadow to some degree, but not entirely, the purposes of God) and reflection on the truths of revelation (which tell us how to share in the life of God). Of course, morality depends upon such questions of fact. How else is one supposed to decide what is the rational way to act? C's own view seems, despite all his praise of autonomy, to rely on a form of wholly arbitrary intuitionism, whereby we just recognize some ways of life to be of unconditioned authority. He cannot justify that opinion, or show it to be rational at all. Then he seeks to make a virtue out of desperation, and say that any attempt at justification would be immoral, since it would undermine the unconditioned authority of the so-called 'religious requirement'.

It is, after all, C who wants the unjustifiable, arbitrary, sheer command of the religious requirement. The traditional theist wants to formulate a reasonable set of rules for action, in view of the facts of human existence and nature.

But, you may protest, must we not just do what is right for its own sake; 'duty for duty's sake', not for any reward? And is the way of the cross not far beyond any merely rational morality? Is all this talk of a reasonable calculation of possibilities not redolent of hidden selfishness and mere prudence? I think that this sort of existentialist agonizing lies behind much of what C says. Duty commands, but offers no rewards; ours is not to criticize in the light of mere reason, but to obey. Is it not ironic that C turns out to be the apostle of heteronomy after all? The subordinator of human freedom, grovelling odiously before stern and unbending Duty? This is the return of prep-school morality with a vengeance: 'Do not ask; obey—and the more it hurts, the better'.

In this whole way of thinking about morality there is a nest of confusions. Of course it is true that, having established what is right, we should do it, despite the temptations of pleasure and laziness. We should do it because it is right; but how do we establish that it is right? Different philosophers, people holding very different world-views, will differ on this question. But it is a very plausible view that the 'right' act is that which is the most reasonable, in view of certain desires and purposes, the sort of act most conducive to maximizing desired ends. But the theist would add a third sort of 'reasonableness' to the two already distinguished. There is self-interested or prudential reason, which asks what will maximize the ends that I desire. There is impartial or just reason, which asks what will maximize the desires of a set of people. For the theist, however, there is also what we may call transcendent or value-centred reason. Transcendent reason asks what will maximize the ends that God, the perfect being, desires or wills.

As we have seen, the commitment to God is not a criterionless commitment, without any reason. It is faithfulness to supreme value; that is, to an existent being who is supremely valuable, not just to some imagined but non-existent ideal state. The key to this faithfulness is love: the longing, reverence and desire to co-operate with, another. If our most reasonable desire is to share in God's life, then we wish to share in his love, to love and be loved by God. We will admire him, respect him and (since we cannot help a supreme being in himself) co-operate, if possible, in realizing his purposes for the world. This is not prudence; it is the disinterested desire for a supremely worthwhile existent object; it is the supremely rational love.

As many philosophers have pointed out, not all our desires need be self-regarding. We can desire to help others; we can desire to be just or virtuous. So we can desire God; acknowledging his supreme perfection, we can want to be like him and to help his purposes. Thus it turns out that the most reasonable, the right, act is what God wills— not as an arbitrary command addressed to our grovelling fear; but as his good purpose, which our love motivates us to realize. It is essential to this view that God objectively exists, that he is not just the imaginary projection of our own goals and ideals. For we cannot really love a non-existent ideal. We can pursue it, but it may prove too difficult and impractical, and we may come, after sad experience, to pay it only a wistful, nostalgic, occasional regard. God cannot fade or become less important in that way. He really exists, and can realize his purposes; he always calls us to co-operate with him by our own unique creative response. There is something we can love, which can love us in return, sustain and empower us as well as exhort and inspire us. To love and obey him is supremely rational. To disobey him is to turn away from what is truly worthwhile.

So the answer to the question 'Why should we obey God's commands?' is that it is entirely reasonable to love the most desirable being there is, and to do what this most wise and knowledgeable of all beings suggests. God's commands are not arbitrary orders; they are necessarily directed to the supreme good of creatures. That is the purpose, the will of God. And, though it may be known in general by rational reflection on

61

created nature, parts of it may be revealed by God, if and insofar as God shows more fully his own nature and purpose for the universe. There is no moral objection to obeying the commands of an almighty being. For this does not take away our critical reflection or rational argument; we still have to work out what his commands are. But it does assure us that moral commitment of the most serious sort is ultimately rational, and will not be in vain. If there is a God, he is the protector and bulwark of morality, not its enemy and underminer. He ensures that nature really is value-filled and purposive, and makes moral commitment an irreducible and important part of that purpose.

# 6

## Duty and Love

C holds that the objective existence of God can never justify moral commitment. It is, he thinks, a sign of a mature moral attitude that we should just work out for ourselves what is right, without any reference to the commands of a supreme being. Now I agree that, in one sense, we should work out for ourselves what is right; we cannot just accept someone else's word for it, without any critical thought. But I have insisted that we do not just *make up* what is right; we really have to try to find out the truth. If that is the case, then it may be very relevant to refer to the commands of a supreme being, in order to discover the truth in morality. That does not commit us to saying that God's commands are always perfectly clear; or that everybody agrees what God has commanded. Not at all. We first have to ask whether it is likely that God has in fact commanded a certain thing; and then we have to ask how we can apply that command in a situation which may be very different. That takes a lot of thought, and leaves room for a lot of discussion. But if God really has commanded something, we are unlikely to discover the truth without thinking hard about that command. Thinking about God's commands is very important, when we are trying to discover what is true in morality. That does not mean that there can be no morality without God. People are bound to have some moral beliefs, whether or not they believe in God. And I do think that people should do what is right, just because it is right, even if they do not believe in God. But I do think that an exploration of the ultimate presuppositions of serious moral commitment (something we just know we have to undertake, if we are to be true to ourselves) will disclose a necessary ground of all values, willing their realization. And I think that a conscious recognition of that fact will affect some of our important moral perceptions (about our inner striving for ideal values, for example).

Probably what most people think is 'right' in our culture is keeping some general principles of morality: such things as not killing, not lying, not stealing, keeping promises and helping those in need. Such principles are obviously beneficial to the running of society on the whole. They are principles to be backed by the strongest sanctions of approval and disapproval and inculcated into the young. They can seem to be just obviously right, for no other reason than that they are right. Yet reasons can be given for them: that they help society to flourish is one good reason for having them. They are not just commands which we intuit. We can work them out, as conditions of human flourishing, which it is in everyone's interest to keep.

Of course, it may well be in my interest to keep these moral rules, but it will very often not be so in particular cases. Why should I obey them, when it is against my interests? The answer is that it is in the general interest; it is what an impartial judge would will. Yet why should I care about that? Here we do seem to get to a basic assertion that impartial concern for human flourishing is just a good thing. Why be impartial and concerned? Because that is the mark of a rational and sensitive person; insofar as I claim to base my conduct on reasons and am moved by sympathy, impartial concern will remain an ideal for me.

The truth is that we cannot get much further with this. In the end, it seems, I will appeal to some obscure sense that I *ought* to be a sympathetic, rational person; that only thus will I fulfil my proper potentiality as a person; only thus will I be 'true to myself'. Interestingly, when C casts around for some sort of justification for the religious ideal, he says both that it cannot be given one and that we seek it 'because consciousness itself—and perhaps all biological life—is such a teleological striving' (121). That is, it is *in our natures* to strive. It is quite a giveaway. The most pure of us appeals in the end, in however muted a way, to human nature as a justification for moral conduct.

For a thoroughgoing atheist, there is no such thing as a *proper* human nature, we are a product of random forces, with no purpose or teleological end; there is no one way in which we ought to live or be. But for a theist, we are created for a purpose: to become, by our own free response, a certain sort of being, rational, sympathetic and creative. The basic 'ought', which underlies human life, is this pressure towards a future possible state, a state, which is the natural outcome of a properly directed life. We are under no necessity to justify the 'ought'; it may remain as an unquestioned obligation. But it can be justified by showing that human nature is made in order to achieve that end, by its own free response. Then the 'ought' is not just an arbitrary or unaccounted feature of the universe. It becomes part of an integral, rational structure, in which rational beings are drawn towards an ideal, which is their true fulfilment. That ideal really exists, as the ideal pattern in the mind of God, which draws them to itself, but it does not restrict human life in a bad sense, as though everyone had to be exactly the same. We can each fill out the ideal in our own way; indeed, part of the idea is that we should each maximize our own individuality. Yet the general structure of this ideal must be the same for all; we are all meant to be rational, sympathetic and creative in some appropriate way. What theism can add to the moral life is this idea of human nature as 'meant' or 'intended' to be a certain way; and the assurance of the possibility of fulfilment.

The position is that we certainly know what states are of value, in general; and we know that some values are more important than others, even if it is difficult always to judge between them in every case. The idea of value is quite independent of religious belief, and it has to be used in thinking what sort of being God, the supremely valuable being, could be. There is no reduction of value to mere fact, or to a value-neutral set of commands. But, even though we know what values are, which values should we aim at in our own situations? And how seriously? And with what chance of success?

An atheist might (though he need not) say: 'I agree that rationality, sympathy and so on are values; that it is good to have knowledge and to help one another. I quite see that. But I need not choose such values; or at least I can choose to pursue them only so far, for so many people, for only some of the time. There is no reason why I should take them so seriously that I have to pursue all of them to the fullest possible extent. In fact, in a world like this, that would be very unrealistic, since it has no chance of success. I will use reason so far as it does not conflict too far with my own interests. I will be sympathetic to my family and friends. In short, I will adjust my pursuit of values to help my pursuit of my own interests. For these are values, too, and I choose them.'

The point is that this is a perfectly reasonable attitude for an atheist; there is little to be said against it, except that it is immoral. But it is precluded for the theist; for him, such a view cannot be reasonable. For the theist, there exists a being of supreme value. We cannot but revere and admire such a being, any more than we can refuse to admire beautiful music or paintings. In God, all the values we acknowledge do not remain as mere possibilities; they are realized in a maximal way. God has created us so that we find our proper fulfilment in realizing some of these values in ourselves and the world around us. We *should* realize them because that is what we are meant, intended, designed, to do. It is absurd to say that we could or should object to such a design, if we accept that the design is by an absolutely perfect being. No moral rebellion against such a being is conceivable. If a perfect being has a specific purpose, then that purpose must exist for the best, wisest and most morally valuable reason. So it is necessarily true that we ought to accept it for ourselves, on pain of foolishness or immorality.

This purpose of God is not just something externally imposed upon us, as though he could have given us quite a different purpose. It is human nature itself which is purposive in its constitution; its proper form of being is the realization of its distinctive powers and potentialities. The special feature of human life is that humans do not just naturally tend to realize their powers, as though they were instinctive. They have the freedom to realize their distinctive possibilities or to acquiesce, instead, in the search for animal pleasure or the deference of others. The natural tendency becomes an 'ought', when one can be deflected from it by passion or ignorance. In that situation, God's purpose becomes a command; though command is a slightly misleading word. It might be better to speak of it as an inspiring ideal or guiding wisdom. It is a command, because when we realize that the fulfilment of our natural tendency is God's purpose, which we are tempted to be deflected from, then his will becomes an obligation upon us, a command by one with supreme authority, that is, perfect knowledge, wisdom and goodness. We should obey one whom we acknowledge to have supreme authority, whether or not he attaches rewards or punishments to our obedience. The reference to rewards and punishments is a red herring.

How could one possibly turn away from such an authority and purpose? This is the ultimate mystery of human sin; the Bible asserts it as a fact, but gives no clear explanation of it. The story of the Garden of Eden suggests that it has to do with disbelief in

God's promises and the desire for God-like knowledge (Gen. 3.4-5). In the Indian tradition the 'fall' is conceived as being due to ignorance or desire. The fact is that belief in God is not just a matter of intellectual agreement that there is a perfect being. It is a matter of actual living relationship to such a being. So whereas it is certainly true that it is only reasonable to assent morally to the purposes of a perfect being, one's actual relationship to that being may lead to rebellion and dissatisfaction. His very omnipotence, which should be seen as the assurance of good, may be experienced as a cloying and confining oppression. His omniscience, the guarantee of wisdom, may be experienced as a prying and unbearable eavesdropping. His will, which shows the way to life and fulfilment, may be experienced as a tyrannical and repressive dictatorship. C seems to take this experience of God, the experience of him by a sinful and rebellious creature, to be the norm of relationship to a real, objective God. He seems to have no sense of the freedom and liberation which can come from knowing that one is created, loved and accepted by a supremely good being, growing knowledge of whose infinite goodness leads to literally endless fulfilment. God is the object of supreme love and he makes supreme love possible for creatures. But that is only so for one whose being is open to love. 'Many waters cannot quench love, neither can floods drown it. If a man offered for love all the wealth of his house, it would be utterly scorned'; thus does the Song of Solomon (8.7) eulogize love, in a passage which has always been taken to picture man's love for God and God's love for man. Such love is worth almost any sacrifice; in it lies the fulfilment of all natural human tendencies; 'the heart is restless till it finds its rest in you', says Augustine. But love is a matter of real living relationship; the heart must be conformed to love, to self-transcendence in the just perception of the other. If the heart cannot yet love; if it still seeks its own good to the exclusion of the other; if it resents the other as a threat or despises it as an object to be used; if it is locked in self-concern; then all the intellectual knowledge in the world cannot make it subordinate itself to the requirement of self-transcending love, which the existence of the supremely valuable being makes upon it; that is, cannot make it obey God.

It is in vain to seek the rewards of love by taking the path of self-concern. If we try to obey God for fear of hell or even out of the desire for heaven, self-concern has not yet lost its insidious grip. Anyone who desires heaven above all things will never attain it. It may seem that the only people who want to get to heaven will never get there, while heaven will be filled with people who did not want to go at all. The truth is a bit more subtle, of course. Heaven is the presence of God; so it is possible to want heaven, insofar as one wants God. It is possible to fear hell, insofar as one wants to avoid losing God. In this sense, it is right to fear hell and desire heaven; but only because what you are really wanting is God. It will never be right just to obey God because you want to be happy for ever or are afraid of suffering. Once again C misrepresents the position dreadfully when he says that it is important not to believe in immortality, if one is to avoid spiritual vulgarity and immaturity (10). The Christian view of immortality has always been that heaven is the presence of God; its inhabitants are those who love God. It is not a reward for those who love themselves or whose moral commitment is merely a more subtle form of long-term prudence. It should be pretty clear to anyone who reads the New Testament that heaven cannot be attained by good works, but only by faith (though good works are a natural consequence of faith, and a test of its genuineness). Faith is a life of trusting belief in God's promises; commitment to him as an object of love, particularly through the personal presence of Jesus Christ. It is openness to the love of God; it is the only inner disposition which can enable one to experience the life of God, poured out for the world in the incarnation.

Hell, on the other hand, is not just a punishment for bad works; that would ignore the doctrine of the forgiveness of sins, the very reason for the death of Christ, the heart of Christian faith. It is the absence of God; its inhabitants (if any) are those who hate God and who cannot experience him as other than a prying, repressive and confining alien power, however much their intellects may tell them that he is a perfect being. It is the natural destiny of those who cannot escape from the circle of fear and hatred which is themselves.

Thus heaven and hell are not external rewards and punishments for good or bad conduct. What they show is the final destiny of those who love or hate God. They do show that love and selfishness have ultimate, important consequences. But they cannot have the function of getting people to love out of long-term selfishness; that would be self-refuting. You could say that they were just irrelevant to the question of moral conduct, but that would not be quite right. They are relevant, but not at the level of providing a selfish reason for being unselfish. They are relevant, because they show that the purposes of the perfect being can indeed be realized and that human fulfilment is possible for all; and they show that evil will not triumph, but will be finally defeated.

People can know intellectually that they are created by a perfect being, in order to find their proper fulfilment in loving him and that failing to love him will result in disintegration, isolation and death. Yet they can fail to love him, because they become trapped in their own self-centredness; and these desires feed the ignorance, weakness and perversion of intellect and will which lead to rejection of God, even as an intellectual theory. So the doctrines of God, heaven and hell cannot be wheeled out as theories which justify morality prudentially. They are not moral doctrines; they state the facts that there is a supremely valuable being, and that one's relation to him will determine one's ultimate destiny. Yet such facts are relevant to morality. They provide a context, a view of the universe and of human nature, which makes sense of seeing morality in terms of absolute demands. These demands are not just issued by individuals themselves, as free decisions (why could they not, like C's arbitrary God, decree *anything* for themselves?); nor do they float around a value-neutral materialistic universe as quite unexplained, as especially queer entities or non-entities. Rather, the moral demands can be coherently seen as objective principles legislated by a being of the highest possible moral authority, with the purpose of achieving the interior purpose of human existence. It will be morally right to obey his commands, as long as we can be fairly sure they are his commands and can have the confident hope that their ultimate point — the fulfilment of human life — will be realized; so our commitment will not be in vain.

So what about the view that moral rules are right anyway, whether or not there is a God? It is quite true and should be accepted; after all, we do not want to encourage sincere atheists to be immoral. We can be fairly sure about some moral obligations, whatever our factual beliefs, and we certainly ought to accept them. I would strongly accept that we are more sure of our obligations than we are of any philosophical justification for them. Yet that does not mean that justification is irrelevant. I am not satisfied with offering no justification, and I think that some proposed justifications are too weak for what we actually believe about the seriousness of obligations. Their acceptance could, though it should not, undermine the seriousness of our first-order moral beliefs. I believe that the objective existence of God provides the most adequate justification for moral beliefs; it certainly does not undermine them. For it allows values to retain their full and irreducible force. It provides for them an intelligible placing in the universe; namely, in the mind of God, as necessary constituents of his being. It gives them an intelligible relation to human nature and its natural tendencies and possibilities; for they are the archetypal ideals towards which human being is naturally orientated. It also relates them intelligibly to the world of nature, for they are not just ideals, without relation to a neutral world; rather, they will inevitably be realized in the world by God's power. In these ways, God helps to explain and safeguard the authority of ethics. For one's general view of the nature of the universe will make a place for ethical demands. It will add force to the seriousness of their pursuit, as one tries to love and obey God, and it will prevent our commitment to morality from being undermined by the cynicism, which can arise from a perception of the persistent failure to realize moral ideals in oneself and others.

Not only will theism safeguard morality, by making sense of moral obligations within a wider structure of being. It will actually affect morality in some important respects. Although Christians do not believe that God sends down a set of clear commands by private telephone, they do believe that God's will is not wholly obscure. On the contrary, it has been decisively revealed in Christ, in his life and teachings. There is great scope for our interpretation of what we see in Christ and our application of it to contemporary problems, but there is still an irreducible datum of revelation there, preserved in the Gospels and elaborated in the great church traditions. We should, as Christians, expect Christians to be rather clearer about God's will, at least in some areas of life, than other people. So we should expect some moral differences, even though the general moral rules, about killing, stealing and so forth, will be generally agreed.

The main difference is perhaps that the life of Jesus and the teachings of the Sermon on the Mount will place before us an ideal of self-giving love, self-denial and purity of attitude that will be absolutely binding, not merely an optional extra. We will need to strive for the virtues of patience, tolerance, joy and thankfulness as divine requirements. The intensity and inwardness of this ideal can only derive from God's revelation in Christ. C himself is very much concerned to safeguard what he calls the 'religious requirement' as the very heart of Christianity. It is, he says, more than a moral requirement, since morals are much more an affair of reasonable compromise. It demands absolute purity and dispassionate love. Yet, he refuses to ground this commitment on any revelation. It must, he says, stand by its own intrinsic authority. I can see that, if one does not believe in an objective God, there is nothing else upon which it can stand; but I cannot, for the life of me, see why there is any plausible reason to accept such a demanding, uncomfortable and, as far as this world goes, impossible ideal as that of Jesus, just for its own sake. There is not much to be said to somebody who, like C, just says that you must do it for no reason; but that will hardly be convincing to people who like their conduct to be reasonable, even if uncomfortable and demanding.

For someone who believes there is a God, who is perfectly good and wise and who meets the highest demands of one's own moral insights and goes beyond them, it is quite rational to suppose that God could reveal his will for humanity in a special way. He does not command this way for its intrinsic authority, whatever that is. I really doubt if that notion makes sense, except as a hangover from a rejected authoritarian form of theism. He commands it, because it is the appropriate way to human fulfilment and because that is the way human life ought to be and what it was intentionally created to be — its true nature. To believe this, we have to believe that human nature was intentionally created, that it can achieve the fulfilment for which it was created, and that Jesus does show that fulfilment in his own life and promise it to us. This is not turning morality into prudence. It is something that shows this moral commitment to be reasonably grounded on the facts of human nature, and that its goal and purpose are possible. We still have to make the commitment; but at least we can see that it is a reasonable one, in the light of God's revelation in Christ. It is when we see God's saving action in Christ and hear his promises of salvation and of fulfilment for all human life, that we commit ourselves to the way of the cross, the way to discover our true selves.

Religion, the Christian religion, is not, as C claims, just a very peculiar, unjustifiable sort of moral commitment, a totally non-rational leap into a way of self-denial, without hope of future fulfilment. That would be a religion of cross without resurrection, denial without salvation, demand without promise. The Christian religion is the preaching of a completed act of deliverance in history and the promise of future fulfilment; it is the preaching of the love of God, revealed in Christ. It is because of that love that we must take up our cross, deny ourselves and follow him; and if we share in his passion, we hope to share also in his glory. We must love, because he first loved us. The Christian life is a response to love declared and made available. In a sense, considerations of reason or human autonomy become irrelevant here. It is not reason which moves us, but the force of love, and when we respond to love freely given, we do not pause to insist on our pathetic autonomy. 'I am my beloved's and my beloved is mine'; when such love speaks, 'the flowers appear on the earth, the time of singing has come' (Song of Solomon). Of course it is reasonable to respond to true love, to give oneself wholly to the beloved, to find renewal of life in love. Yet reason seems too weak a name; we do not love for reasons that we can specify, even when love is reasonable. We do not protest about loss of autonomy when we give ourselves up wholly to the loved one. It is when, and perhaps only when, we see the objective reality, the cost and the beauty of the love of God for us, that we can be finally released from the terrible misperception that he is a devouring tyrant or a threat to freedom. Then we will see the reasonableness of commitment to the way and ideal of Christ. It is not a coolly calculating prudence nor is it a blind self-assertion; it is the flight of the loved one to the source and ultimate object of all love. That is the reality of God; when rightly seen, it does draw from us a total commitment and self-offering.

One of the saddest things about C's book, is his total lack of any sense of the beauty of the divine love. For him, our commitment and denial is just to a way of life which we choose; it is directed to the quieting of our own souls. Christian commitment, however, must be to God; it must be directed in response to God's love; that is the only way in which the paradoxical biblical statements about finding joy even in self-denial make any sense. For the self-denial is not just a repression of self in the face of a neutral, uncaring nature; it is a free and joyful giving of self to the one whose love called it into being, and who now calls it to eternal companionship.

So, for the Christian, morality in its deepest sense is the transformation of the heart by love; not our own love, but God's love. That turns stern duty into the delight of loving service; and makes the Christian life a passionate attempt to be like its master, and so to grow into the mind of Christ. Not only do Christians have a binding ideal; they have a distinctive approach to morality. For they aim to rely on grace and on God's own love to transfigure their efforts. The Christian life does depend upon the truth that God gives his life in Christ and this will give new life, force and intensity to the pursuit of moral values.

Naturally, there are other ways in which Christian belief will impinge upon morality, usually by affecting our general attitudes or predispositions, which have been moulded by response to God's revelation in Christ. Thus people may come to believe that God calls them to a specific job or function. That call will become binding upon them, even though such things cannot be matters of moral rules in general. With regard to specific moral issues, too, we might not have exact answers to every question; nor should we expect agreement among all Christians; there probably never has been such agreement, from the time of the first arguments among the apostles, recorded in Acts. But Christians will clearly be disposed to regard the sanctity of human life with special reverence, since it is created by God and in his image. They will tend to view sexuality as primarily expressive of that personal and faithful love which marks the relation of God to his people. They will be sceptical of political policies, which assume the perfectibility of man or which treat individual lives as means to ends. They will regard violence and war as, at best, regrettable necessities, which should be mitigated as far as possible by mercy and compassion, especially for the innocent. Such basic predispositions are often important, and a Christian faith will ensure that they mark the reflective decisions which are necessary in the complexities of moral practice. There is no danger here that faith will lead to an over-simplification of complex issues. Indeed, if Christianity has been criticized in the past, it is for the opposite vice of too much casuistry, too much attention paid to particular cases. On the contrary, there is a full preservation of human reason and the necessity for sensitive reflection and attention to complicated facts; there is also the insistence that what is being sought is the fulfilment of human life, full respect for persons as images of God, and the rule of justice and mercy in society.

In conclusion, I deny completely that 'the authority of morality in no way depends upon questions of fact' (67), and that no fact can be of religious or moral relevance. I assert, in total opposition to C, that God is an almighty individual whose will creates the religious requirement (cf. his denial, in those words, on p. 85)—though I would rather say that it is God's love which arouses the religious response of loving commitment. C simply does not consider the way in which most philosophers have always felt the need to make sense of morality by placing it in an intelligible factual context. He fails to see that one can preserve the irreducibility of moral values in general, while maintaining that certain moral obligations, or certain predispositions towards moral issues, may be matters of divine command. That is because he seems to have no idea at all of how the existence of a supremely loving creator will arouse, in those who are able to respond to his love, a supremely committed obedience, freely given. C objects to an odious grovelling before an arbitrary despot. He prefers a stern self-commitment to the way of self-denial, without real hope of success or reward. There is another way. It is a way made possible for the first time by the perception of the love of God, which awakens in us all the joy and longing and devotion of the enraptured heart. To obey that God; to receive from his hand what he is pleased to give; to be raised up by him to share in his life; what more could one ask? 'This is my beloved and my friend; he is altogether desirable' (Song of Solomon). If such a being commands me, I will gladly obey; because without him, once he has been seen, everything is empty and vain.

# 7

## Faith and Fact

What is the relevance of historical claims to the gospel of salvation? Salvation, according to C, consists in a 'maximal degree of liberation from the power of evil and of spiritual individuation, creativity and responsiveness . . . Compared with this tremendous religious reality,' he says, 'historical claims about walking corpses and empty tombs are foolish and irrelevant' (45).

This sounds all right at first glance, but let us examine it further. The 'power of evil' is, or includes, I suppose, human impulses to anger, hatred, intolerance and fear, which poison and destroy human relationships. So to be 'saved' would be to be in full control of one's emotional life; to be a creative and sensitive individual, expressing one's gifts and caring for others, happy and wise. Certainly that is a very desirable state. Now how is history relevant to it?

First of all, it is highly relevant to ask if such a state is possible. The answer, derived from long and sad historical experience, seems to be that it is not. A very few people come somewhere near it. Many more improve slowly by aiming at it. Most find it totally beyond them. History corroborates the Christian doctrine of sin, the distance of humans from salvation and their inability to achieve it. Where, then, is the gospel? Is it merely the disclosure of an impossible ideal? Hardly; there is not much gospel in that. The gospel is that, despite appearances, salvation is attainable; 'The Kingdom is at hand', Jesus preached. It is not fully attainable here and now, but its attainment is promised, and the sure way to it can begin now.

But who promises it? And can he be trusted? Now history comes in again to tell us that Jesus promised it; even C admits this, when he says, 'Salvation was attained by Jesus'. But how does he know that, without a reference to history? Certainly, a promise could be trusted, if it is made by one who has himself attained salvation and has the power to bring it to others, but these are historical questions. Has Jesus attained salvation? Has he the power to bring it to others? The testimony of the apostles is that he was without sin, so close to the Father as to be one with him; and that by his resurrection he shows that he can overcome the powers which hold us back. The sinlessness and the resurrection of Jesus are historical facts which are essential to establishing that salvation is possible for us after death, brought by the sinless one who has gone before us. If those claims are false, we have no sure promise of salvation. If that is so, salvation becomes an impossible ideal. It can be quickly given up, as a pleasant but impractical dream, to be forgotten amid the harsher realities of the real world.

Salvation must be real; it must be historical. There is no gospel, if there is no historical resurrection. But, C says, we can enjoy salvation through Jesus—and that *is* faith in his resurrection. This is completely false. We cannot *now* fully enjoy salvation; if there is no afterlife, we can *never* enjoy it. The most we could hope for would be an increase in love or joy or peace. That is certainly something. Christianity would become a movement for moral improvement, but it would certainly not offer escape from bondage to sin. Furthermore, what is meant by enjoying salvation 'through Jesus'? If it means, by the real indwelling power of the risen Lord, that presupposes the resurrection and the unique place of Jesus among men in relation to God. But if it only means something like 'inspired by Jesus' example', then it implies nothing about resurrection at all. It seems to me that what we may better say is that we begin to experience the transforming power which will lead to our salvation, as the risen Christ makes himself known to us. There is here a clear four-fold historical claim—that our life is transformed; that we will be saved; that Christ was raised from death; and that it is he who now works in us. Of these, C keeps only the first; and that is the weakest of all, for such transformation is not usually too obvious to the uninitiated.

C might not be so scathing about 'walking corpses and empty tombs', if he saw how such claims are no more than particular examples of the sorts of historical fact which must be true, if our hopes of salvation through Christ are not to be founded on illusion. It sounds all right to say that what matters is my spiritual state now, not what may or may not have happened two thousand years ago. It is all right, until we reflect that my spiritual state does not exist in a historical vacuum. It depends on the whole web of related factors which have made it possible, stretching back genetically through my ancestors, socially through the history of my nation, physically through the huge chains of atomic causality, and so on. It is no mere speculation, it is assured fact, that what I am today does depend essentially on what happened two thousand years ago.

The only question is whether historical events surrounding the life of Jesus played an important part in this process. And I think we can be sure they did, at least if my spiritual state has developed within the Christian tradition. What matters most for us is that, if Jesus was not sinless and did not rise from death, then the whole tradition which has shaped our spiritual state is mistaken in important ways. If our lives are transformed, it will not be by the power of Jesus. We will not be able to rely on his promises for salvation, but will have to look elsewhere. We will, in fact, have turned into something else, members of some new religion of our own, perhaps. We will not be Christians. Does that matter? The reason it matters is that, if we are truly to be saved, we must know what salvation is; and we can only truly know what salvation is, if we know what human nature ought to be, and how it may become it. In the end, a view of what human nature is, what the origin and destiny of man is and what our possibilities and limitations are, is presupposed to our attaining salvation. We need never have worked out such a view explicitly for ourselves, but it must be there.

Now some parts of these views are more important than others. If you do not believe in God or in life after death, your view of human possibilities will be very different. You will not see salvation as lying in relation to a personal God, or as capable of completion after death. It will have to be some state of human flourishing in this life. In such a case, my own preference would be for an Aristotelian view that flourishing was possible only for the few and lay in the pursuit of culture. This ideal would be desirable, no doubt, but its pursuit would not be absolutely binding. It would be equally possible to deny altogether that there was such a thing as human flourishing and leave everyone to get on with pursuing their own aims as they could, not assuming that there is any ideal human life at all.

So, of course, my spiritual state does depend upon what I believe about human nature and destiny, upon what I think fulfilment is and how it may be achieved. Now the Christian does not just believe in God in general. He believes that God makes his own life available in the fellowship of those who pray for the power of the risen Christ, the Church. The Church is not a free-floating organization, unattached to past history. It grows from one historical context; it lives by, the presently enacted remembrance of the life of Christ. The reason why past history is important is that one historical person, Jesus, showed what salvation was and how it was to be achieved. He founded the Church as his body, a growing historical organization that was to be related integrally to him and to be the proper means of conveying salvation to the world. If God did not then so act, then our whole present understanding of salvation is mistaken.

This is corroborated by the fact that C's own non-historical understanding of salvation is markedly different from the orthodox Christian account; that is, he recommends us to aim at a spiritual state in which a living belief in Christ would not result. It is, as he perceives, more Buddhist than Christian. But it is certain that most Buddhists would reject it as vehemently as most Christians would. Now it may be that C has in fact managed to disentangle superstition from true religion at last, and has discovered that all present religions are superstitious, so that he needs to start a new one. We must assess the sort of spiritual state he recommends on its own merits. How, then, does he describe it?

He describes it as a state of 'disinterestedness'; and while he never defines it very carefully, he gives a number of rather different, loose characterizations of it, scattered throughout his book. On p. 76, he speaks of 'the highest degree of dispassionate compassion, selfless self-awareness, and *disponibilité* or attentive and free availability to others'. On p. 86, he speaks of 'a complete and final knowledge, criticism and transformation of himself . . . complete emancipation from fate'. On p. 87, we have perfect 'non-acquisitive non-defensiveness'; and on p. 101, there is 'a kind of quiet watchfulness . . . inner clarity and simplicity'. Finally, on p. 64, he speaks of 'freedom, spiritual autonomy and sovereignty over nature . . . perfect self-possession and fully-achieved spiritual individuality'. In the absence of any systematic description, we will have to make do with these scattered clues.

I will begin by asking this very fundamental question: is absolute disinterestedness the highest sort of spiritual state, the state of salvation or human wholeness? One certainly does find an ideal of total lack of attachment in the Buddhist, and, less unequivocally, in some Hindu, scriptures, but it is noteworthy that the ideal expressed there is based upon precisely that sort of description of the facts, which C despises so much. The 'four holy truths' which are generally accepted as being definitive of Buddhism, are these: first, all is suffering, or unsatisfactory, or such as to give rise to unease. Secondly, the cause of such suffering is desire. Thirdly, the way to the end of suffering is consequently to renounce all desire. Fourthly, the way to renounce desire is through the noble eightfold path, the 'middle way' of moral renunciation and meditation, taught by Gautama Buddha.

Now these are factual, not moral, statements. They do, of course, involve evaluations of the world. To say that everything gives rise to dissatisfaction is certainly an evaluative statement, but it is also meant to be a statement of fact. It is said to be true that everything will eventually produce unease, and one will not be able finally to evade that truth. This is a particularly clear instance of the way in which factual and evaluative statements cannot be as sharply separated from one another as C suggests. What we judge the facts to be, will be inevitably influenced by our own evaluations. It is not always just a matter of getting quite neutral evidence, equally checkable by any number of observers, all of whom will be compelled by that evidence to agree. We have to evaluate the world, in order to make statements about its ultimate character, either to say that it is quite neutral with regard to moral matters, or that it cannot satisfy human desires, or that it can provide a supremely satisfying and meaningful destiny for creatures; but, though we cannot get rid of evaluative elements, we are still trying to state the facts. It was one of the greatest mistakes of Positivist philosophy (now virtually extinct) to suppose that the facts were value-neutral and must always be agreed upon by equally intelligent observers.

If we suppose that the Buddhist assessment of the nature of ultimate reality is true; that the world offers no hope of final satisfaction; and that the Buddha's teaching of renunciation and non-attachment offers the only hope of escape from perpetual unhappiness; then we are likely to adopt the ideal of absolute dis-interestedness, lack of interest in, or desire for, anything. Such an ideal becomes reasonable, if desire will only lead to further suffering for creatures (not for oneself, particularly; since sophisticated Buddhists do not think there is a continuing self to worry about).

There is one and only one book in the Bible which carries a hint that this assessment of the world is true, the book of Ecclesiastes. But its conclusion is still very different from the Buddhists: 'what I have seen to be good and fitting is to eat and drink and find enjoyment . . . the few days of his life which God has given' (5.18). There is no tendency to renounce all desire; the meaning of life must be found in it even for the despairing Teacher of Wisdom. The teaching of Christ is that the supreme meaning lies in love; that, while the world without God indeed offers nothing but final dissatisfaction and despair, a clear knowledge of God would fill the world with meaning and unending delight. Suppose we think that the world, when transformed by clear knowledge of God, does offer the prospect of endless joy; then surely it becomes irrational to say that we should be absolutely uninterested in this, as in anything else. Surely the only rational thing to do is to desire it with all the passion at our disposal, to 'hunger and thirst' after a glimpse of this God, this pearl of infinite value. As in the Buddhist case, this is not a selfish desire, not because the self does not really exist (it does), but because such overwhelming goodness is desired for all creatures. So the ideal will not be total lack of interest, but almost the opposite: total interestedness, commitment to a positive good, passionate involvement to disclose the true object of desire to all, not renunciation of all desires.

There are overlaps between the Buddhist ideal and the Christian. Both are opposed to indiscriminate sensuality, to anger, pride, ignorance and acquisitiveness. Both recommend compassion. Yet the Buddhist compassion is more quiet and reserved, since ultimately each person is master of his own fate and cannot really be helped by others. In one great Buddhist work, the *Dhamma-paddha,* the seeker is told to go off into the forest alone, like a hippopotamus, leaving family and friends, and seek release by contemplation. This is a higher way than the way of works and of the active love which seeks the good of others; and there is no sense at all of the importance of community, of human fellowship as a component of salvation. That is not surprising, since what the Buddhist seeks is extinction, a 'blowing-out' of the flame of desire for life, a solitary submergence into the Absolute, or into Nothingness (it is uncertain which).

Now in the Jewish and Christian traditions there is a quite central stress on the importance of the community, of history and of the value and the goodness of the world. What is to be sought is, ideally, justice in society, which becomes, in Christianity, the communion of saints, the fellowship of all who turn to God. This is a communal thing, unlike the Buddhist liking for solitude. Within such communities, love can flourish, as something different from the Buddhist compassion, which is sorrow for the attachment of beings to the wheel of suffering. Christian love is joy in the desire for one another; it is a delighting and admiring as well as a giving and helping. It is a value to be realized within the world; it is, again unlike the Buddhist ideal, a form of attachment, of interest, of desire.

This is closely related to the Christian stress on the importance of history, a stress completely lacking in the Indian tradition, and which C wishes to reject, too. If salvation is escape from the world; if the world offers only suffering; and if there is no importance in communal life; then history is no more than a sad catalogue of error and despair, without value or importance. But if salvation is the creation of a community of creative and responsive individuals; if human life offers a real fulfilment; if the individuals can only flourish in community; then we need to see in history at least the foreshadowings of such a purpose. We need to know that such salvation is possible. So the people who proclaim it and the historical form of that proclamation become an essential part of the proclamation itself. We may say that the Buddha teaches a way to salvation, but the Christ *is himself* the way to salvation. It does not matter when the teacher lived, or if he ever really lived at all; his teaching, a quite a-historical body of truths, is what matters. But it matters immensely whether the way to salvation lived, and when he lived and how he lived; for what matters is his person and the sort of God it shows.

I suggest, then, that C is wrong in his claim that the requirement of salvation depends upon no factual beliefs about the universe; and his characterization of salvation is really quite distinct from either a Christian or a Buddhist one; it is a sort of arbitrary mixture of elements from both, without any factual doctrines to justify the mix or show it to be reasonable. We know what salvation is, only when and if we see what the appropriate attitude to the ultimate nature of human life and its possibilities is. There is no great merit in just deciding to be absolutely disinterested. Indeed, I have suggested that total lack of interest is a defect, not a virtue, and that we should aim for the orientation of our desires to a wholly appropriate object. That, of course, is God; and, secondarily, all those things which he himself wills for creation, including the fulfilment of all his creatures. C asks repeatedly how belief in a Creator-Mind or in an omniscient being can have religious relevance. The answer should now be clear. The objective existence of God is religiously relevant, because it makes the demand for total love appropriate, rational and authoritative.

Now that does mean that one's commitment to the way of salvation depends upon one's assessment of the facts; it is not just a sort of especially intense moral commitment. We have to know whether God exists, before we can rationally commit ourselves to the way of loving God. That is probably obvious to most people, but C objects to it, on the ground that no piece of merely factual information could logically be the foundation of a total commitment. This is particularly so, when it is metaphysical or historical facts which are in question. For they must always remain disputable and problematic. We should never believe more strongly than the evidence requires. So we can never base a total life-commitment on such uncertain data.

At this point we have come to one of the lynch-pins of C's position. Can we found an absolute faith on a disputed hypothesis? It is always a temptation to philosophers to buy their way out of difficulties by paying an exorbitant price. The price of avoiding this difficulty is to accept that absolute faith is not a matter of truth or falsity at all; so it is not subject to the demands of verification or falsification. Then faith becomes just a commitment to a way of life, neither true nor false; and in that sense beyond dispute.

This price is so high that very few philosophers are prepared to pay it. C sometimes gives the impression that 'modern philosophers' have agreed on a doctrine of religious language, according to which it is not fact-stating, but something else: expressive, commissive or emotive. That would be very far from the truth. One or two philosophers, notably Richard Braithwaite and D. Z. Phillips, have taken such a course, and perhaps one could add A. J. Ayer and R. M. Hare to the list; But there are not many more, and their account is rejected by almost all other philosophers, who have heard of it. Many would not profess to be able to tell what 'religious language' is; many would think it obviously fact-stating, but incoherent or plainly false; and many would think it fact-stating and, in its Christian form, true (three of the five professors of philosophy in Oxford and Cambridge hold that last view at the time of writing, 1982).

Even if faith is supposed to be non-factual, people are still going to disagree about it. They will adopt different sorts of faith or none at all. All C will be able to say is, 'Well, some choose one thing and some another; none of these choices is true or false'. So we could rephrase the difficult question: can we found an absolute faith on a disputed hypothesis? as the similar question: can we reasonably adopt a disputed faith, for which there is nothing more to be said, in an absolute way? If you should not hold any belief more strongly than the evidence suggests, it is equally plausible to maintain that you should not hold any belief which is highly disputed in an irrevocable way.

The trouble is, of course, that such beliefs, which are about the whole orientation of one's life, can hardly be held provisionally. You either commit your life to them or you do not. You may wonder whether to be committed, but once you are, there are no half-measures. Even when you have seen how widely these beliefs are disputed, you have to judge for yourself whether or not to adopt them. Even on C's account, it is surely absurd to adopt a belief for no reason at all. You must ask whether it is reasonable to adopt the belief; and how can you decide *that*, when you realize that equally rational people have made quite different decisions? Would it not follow that the adoption of any belief at all was arbitrary and unjustifiable?

Of course, on my account, you do not judge whether to *adopt* a belief; you have to judge whether it is true. But as far as rationality goes, is it any worse to try to judge whether a belief is true, when its truth is widely disputed, than to try to decide whether it is rational to adopt a way of life, when its rationality is widely disputed? I do not think so; in which case even C's price gives an empty victory. The view that he is taking has its antecedents in Lessing's rationalism, which saw faith as a matter of eternal truths and protested that such truths could not be founded on contingent matters of historical fact. Morality, or the extreme form of it which he calls the 'religious requirement', is more certain than the truth of any metaphysical speculation or historical judgement, he seems to be claiming. But is it? It would only be plausible to say so, if there was complete agreement among all rational and sincere disputants, but there is not. In fact, C is in a tiny minority among moralists and religious believers, as he would have to confess. Can we commit ourselves to a widely disputed faith or way of life? If not, out goes the religious requirement. If so, then we can equally rationally commit ourselves to a widely disputed metaphysical theory or alleged historical fact. Either way, C is hoist with his own petard.

Nevertheless, we still have to deal with the question: with what certainty can we commit ourselves to a widely disputed set of facts? The model that is set before us is of a group of dispassionate observers, all with nothing to lose from an answer, testing the evidence for some hypothesis. These perfectly rational beings will proportion their beliefs to the strength of the evidence, which is observer-neutral and available to all, and thus will be less confident the more there is dispute among them. The model, in fact, is that of the perfectly rational scientist in the perfect laboratory, seeking a set of fairly clear answers to a set of fairly specific and clearly definable problems.

However, the more we deal with questions involving personal realities, the more we stand to gain or lose much by our answers; the more we are involved with the subject-matter, by our own deepest attitudes and interests, the more dispute there is about the sort of answer for which we are looking, the less the model of the rational scientist applies. Consider economics as an example. Here, we are dealing with the behaviour of persons, trying to predict and explain it to some degree. But there is a lot at stake, which affects us personally, and it is not wholly clear what sort of explanation is to be found, or how far predictions can ever be accurate. So economists differ profoundly over their theories of economic human behaviour, even though they mean their theories to be true—to fit the facts in the best possible way. They might not be certain about their theories; yet they cannot remain neutral, since they must act on some theory. However speculatively unsure they are, they must be practically committed. This is the first important point: in matters of great and unavoidable practical decision, it is necessary to be decisive, even at the risk of error and even when theoretical certainty is not available.

There is another point, too. Some of these disputes are not about clearly specified data, according to agreed criteria of decision-making. They are disputes about what data are relevant, what one should count as a good explanation, or what sort of evidence is required. Such disputes do in fact occur in theoretical sciences, too. Of course, some recourse to facts will ultimately resolve the issue. But it may be a very sophisticated recourse indeed: the kinds of evidence, which a nuclear physicist will use, are so embedded in theory that most people could not see how it is relevant, or even understand the theory to which it is relevant; and it may not be available except under very special conditions—only in laboratories or in ideal economic situations. It is certainly not a matter of just looking and seeing. It is a matter of devising sophisticated theories, arranging specialized conditions and seeing the relevance of this recondite evidence to one's theories. Thus there is evidence for the special theory of relativity, but most of us could not say what it was, or how to obtain it, or whether it really confirms the theory or not, if it was right in front of us. The point here is that the facts are certainly relevant to our theories and to our attempts to get at the truth about the world, but they are not relevant in a simple, straightforward way. It takes a genius to devise a good experimental test for a sophisticated theory; and even then, there might not be a high degree of certainty available, on purely theoretical grounds. Again, however, it is rational for a person to commit his whole life to the assumption that a certain theory is true, even though he may be wrong. It is worth the risk of error; for without risk, there will be no chance of getting the truth. The search for verifying conditions may be difficult and arduous; it may pay off in the end, even though all the indications were against it at first. It is a familiar story in science that the great scientist is at first opposed or ignored by all his contemporaries. Yet science only progresses by his resolute commitment to a theory, which all his peers dispute.

These two points are very relevant to the case of theism. First, I have argued, it should make a great difference to one's life, whether or not one believes in God. This is a matter of practical urgency. If theoretical certainty is unobtainable either way, one cannot refuse to commit oneself. You must either live as if God exists, or as if he does not. You must either pray or not, seek salvation or not, obey his commands or not, and love him or not. In this situation, it is rational to commit oneself, even on the basis of a small probability; there is simply no alternative.

Secondly, theism is a highly general and wide-ranging theory about the nature of all reality. The tests for it are difficult to devise; and there are disputes about what would finally verify it and the relation of evidence to the theory. I myself think that a life after death, in which a growing knowledge of God is possible, would verify theism. I think that experiences of God's presence now—experiences of the world as moral, purposive and personal—tend to verify it. But there are also the disconfirming experiences of evil and of the apparent absence of God at times, or to many people. So verification is not a simple, straightforward issue. In this situation, it is rational for a person to take the risk of committing his whole life to the verification of God—that is, to seeking closer knowledge and love of God—even when opposed by rational contemporaries, and when one may in fact be wrong. So we are not claiming a dispassionate speculative certainty nor basing our lives on such a thing. We are taking a bet that the universe is ultimately personal, valuable and purposive; we are living as if that were true, on the basis of some positive indications, the hope of later more positive indications, and the necessity of taking up some position in the absence of stronger evidence. We start by saying that the hypothesis of God seems true, as far as we can tell. But it becomes so much a part of our practical lives and experience, that we soon have to say that it no longer has the status of a hypothesis, a speculative theory. It is the very foundation upon which we build our lives, a commitment which, while intensely practical, does involve a view of the ultimate nature of the world. For it is not a theory about some external object, with which we are not concerned personally. It is a view about our own deepest natures, about an object to which we relate personally, in love; it is a view which defines what we are.

It seems to me quite wrong to say that we are more certain about moral obligations or the reasonableness of practical commitments than we are of ultimate truths about human nature. In fact, to believe that there are intrinsically obliging moral principles and to decide that certain commitments are reasonable, we must already have some view of what human nature is—whether it is a bundle of macro-molecules, an immaterial soul attached to a body, or a conscious material thing, created by a good God. We know that we cannot be speculatively certain about such views. We know that they are, and seemingly always will be, disputed by intelligent people. But we cannot help having one, for we have to act in view of a specific understanding of ourselves and our own natures. Here, we must seek the truth as best we can, trying to understand the views of others, and constantly rethinking our own in the light of them. But we cannot just give up our own view. So here is a third element in theism. The first was that important commitments sometimes have to be made on small estimates of probability. The second was that very general metaphysical theories can be rationally adopted on the basis of disputed and conflicting evidence. Now the third is that I have to come to some understanding of my own way of being in the world; and at this point, practical commitment and theoretical assessment run inextricably together. I cannot be neutral and dispassionate towards the question of my own being. Nor can I rationally make a practical commitment without any idea of what sort of being I, who am committing my*self*, am. The practice does not precede the theory; and the theory does not precede the practice. It is in taking up a practical attitude that I declare what I am; and it is in discerning what I am, that I take up a practical attitude to myself and my world. Precisely at this point, the fact-value split ceases to exist. I cannot get a value-neutral view of my own being; and my evaluation of myself is not some subjective reaction to a dispassionate account of the facts about me. I only get at the facts by taking up an attitude, and the sort of facts I see will depend on my attitude. Yet my attitude is a response to the facts as I see them.

This may sound impossibly circular; but it is not. It is simply pointing out that, at this point of self-understanding, knowledge, the sort of knowledge appropriate to a personal being, *is* taking up an appropriate dispositional attitude. To know is to react appropriately; and we react appropriately only in knowing truly. At this point, Christian faith prompts the view that we only know truly when our practical commitment is one of love. It is love, affection, concern, that provides us with just perception, appropriate discernment, knowledge of the truth. Conversely, it is knowing the truth that sets us free to love; it is the knowledge of God which shows love to us. Love is cognitive and knowledge is affective. It is a fundamental mistake to separate these aspects of human being completely.

Of course the scientist in the laboratory does not have to love and be personally involved with his electrons. It is not quite so absurd to say that he must have a love for the beauty and elegance of nature, for truth itself and for knowledge. But in our daily lives with one another, it becomes more apparent that we can know and understand better the things which we love or with which we sympathize. In personal relationships, we can only really understand other persons when we can love them to some degree. Our love does reveal new things about them to us, and our knowledge does lead us to relate to them in new ways. It may not be always quite true that to understand is to forgive. But at least, to understand is to appreciate more; and understanding is only possible where some appreciation begins to exist.

Nothing is more obvious in human life than the way in which our feelings for other people govern our assessments of them. We do try to make 'objective' assessments of people. But, if we are honest, we will agree that a completely objective assessment is a human impossibility and is not even desirable. For there are facts about personal beings which can only be disclosed to non-objective, highly affective, vision. There are things which can only be known by love.

Now the basic theistic claim is that the fundamental nature of reality is personal. If that is true, it will be the case that its fundamental nature can only be known by love, and will be hidden from those whose affective attitudes are disorientated by sin. Since, on the Christian view, we are all to some extent disorientated by sin, knowledge of God will not be a natural possibility. It will be, in short, a matter of grace. That does not mean that God arbitrarily selects those who will know him. It does mean that, if God's being is personal, knowledge of it will depend both upon our affective attitude to it (and so to the world which expresses it), and upon his self-disclosive activity. It means that a general knowledge of God will be obscured or distorted by sin; so that it will need to be corrected by the divine self-revelation. Such revelation will necessarily be particular and historically limited, as all expressions of personal being must be unique and particular. A true knowledge of God will come to those who are open to the power of love, and who attend to his revelation in history. Such knowledge need not be absolutely exclusive or exhaustive, but it will be the most adequate form of knowledge open to us. If God is truly personal, then the form of his revelation will be particular and unique and personal; and it cannot be compromised by an allegedly tolerant mixing with other faiths, which have a non-personalist view of the ultimate nature of reality, like Buddhism.

Such an attitude may seem to be tolerant, but in fact it is not tolerant at all. For it amounts to saying that Buddhists are wrong, if they keep to their traditional understanding, just as Christians are wrong, if they keep to theirs. It is no very great tolerance to inform all the interested parties that they are equally wrong, so they can be tolerated as equally superstitious. It might indeed be less arrogant not to try to tell believers what they really believe, or ought to believe, and just to accept their own accounts.

Now nobody with any sense is going to say that Buddhism, as such, is just mistaken, any more than anyone could say that Christianity, in all its many forms, with all its complex doctrines, is mistaken, or correct either. You have to take particular doctrines one by one, and ask how they may either represent similar insights seen in different cultures, or how they do reflect basically differing views about reality. If you do this, I expect the Christian will find many particular Buddhist insights to reflect some of his own. He will, if he is wise, find some truths in Buddhism which he can embrace as widening his own vision. What he cannot do, is to say that the basic truths of his own faith, about the personalness of God, the salvation of the world in Christ, and the immortality of the human individual, are actually false, just because Buddhists disagree with them. There just *are* basic disputes in religion. And, while one should try to learn from others and understand them, one cannot believe contradictory things at once. C's attempt to have a 'Christian Buddhism' is a misconceived attempt at tolerance which only succeeds in offending all the people to whom he is trying to be tolerant.

However, there is one other important thing that should be said. If God is personal, there will be an important sense in which knowledge of him cannot be put into words. There are many things that we know about ourselves and others which we cannot describe: our feelings, our attitudes, even our deepest beliefs. We have what has been called 'knowledge by acquaintance', which is very real, but not expressible in blunt prose. We may sometimes express it in poetry or music, but personal emotional life cannot be captured by the precise, dispassionate prose of natural science. For this reason, it is misleading to see Christian or religious doctrine just as a matter of precise philosophical theories. It is, I think, arguable, that one of the great defects of the Western Christian tradition has been the attempt to codify beliefs in clear and precise and dispassionate formulae. Far more important are the symbols and metaphors and poetry and narratives which express a sense of a living relationship with God, but are not expressible in clear propositions. The central Christian rite, the

Eucharist, is a very good example of the way in which symbols can move deeply and express truths about the relation of God and man, without ever being adequately capturable in any set of doctrines. If this is so, one will not place too high a value on precise formulations of doctrine. For religion is not primarily philosophy, but a living relationship with God. Yet it would be quite wrong to say that religious language is therefore *just* expressive, as though it did not state facts at all. When, in the liturgy, we say, 'This is my body', it may be very difficult to say exactly what facts we state. But it is giving up the ghost entirely to say we are not asserting any facts, but only expressing our feelings about pieces of bread. Symbolism is important, because what is ultimately at stake is acquaintance with a personal God, and that is never exhaustively describable. But there are true and false doctrines about God: he does love us and does not hate us; and they are presupposed to our having any personal experience of God at all.

Suppose now that we return to our question: with what certainty can we commit ourselves to a widely disputed set of facts? We can now see that certain sorts of knowledge are identical with, or at least inseparable from, the adoption of basic attitudes to ourselves and the world. Personal knowledge is inseparable from evaluation. So we necessarily commit ourselves to certain cognitive beliefs when we take up specific attitudes to things. It is not so much a question of theoretical certainty, as a practical necessity to orient ourselves in the world in one way or another. There is no backing out of such commitment. The most we can do is try to ensure that our commitment is as rational as we can make it—that we have wide knowledge of the facts, extensive sympathy and a true grasp of the relative importance of the various data presented to us.

If that to which we are basically committing ourselves as theists, is a living relationship to a person or to the world apprehended as expressive of personhood, then just as important to us as doctrinal disputes will be the efficacy of the symbols and stories of the faith to evoke and sustain in us such a relationship. The life of Jesus; the parables of Jesus; the images which have been built around the person of Jesus by reflection; the rites and symbols of the Church; the subtle and moving narratives of the people of Israel: these are the things which may open our eyes to depths in human life and guide our apprehension of those depths, whether or not we can intellectually formulate our vision and understanding.

In other words, we are not primarily dealing with a theory, even though some theories must be presupposed by our way of life. We are dealing with a certain sort of apprehension and sensitivity, an ordering of importances and an orientation of attitudes, which takes place below (or perhaps beyond) the level of intellect. The religious vision of the world as symbol and sacrament is something which can be evoked, but never inferred. It is a matter of perception, commitment and evaluation, indissolubly bound together in the response of the whole person to the complex whole of his experienced world. Theism is not a hypothesis, even though it presupposes a hypothesis. It is a total reaction to the world, seen under an irreducible and distinctive aspect, the aspect of transcendent reality, which is opened to us, but not described, by the symbols and narratives of a tradition of faith.

Religions offer us images of transcendence; by using them, we evoke a sense of transcendence in ourselves. If that happens, then our metaphysical theories and our assessment of historical probabilities will have to be such as to take account of the presence of transcendent reality within our world. The old rationalist question, 'How can I found an absolute faith on mere metaphysical or historical probabilities?' is misconceived. Faith is not founded on the assessment of such probabilities at all. It is founded on the way of worship and prayer, which discloses to us the world as expressive of transcendent reality. It is founded on the symbols, images, narratives and personal lives which open up for us a sense of that reality. It is only when we have been touched by that vision that we can go on to explore its implications for metaphysics and history. Then we construct metaphysical doctrines of God to try to work out the relation of the transcendent to the world, but always to a degree tentatively, certainly with regard to details. Then we ask how our vision originated in history, and assess historical probabilities anew, in the light of the fact that history does express the transcendent. Now we may begin to take seriously the claim of the Jewish people to discern God in history, and to be the mediators of his revelation to the world. Once we take seriously the possibility that God may disclose himself in history, our assessment of history is likely to differ markedly from that of an atheist. So, while faith is not founded on our assessment of historical probabilities, nevertheless our faith did originate in certain historical circumstances. The truth of certain religious beliefs may depend upon the truth of certain historical occurrences. If salvation, conceived as the fulfilment of human nature by relation to a personal God, is made possible for us and promised to us by the work and person of Jesus Christ, then its possibility and actuality do depend upon facts about Jesus: that he lived, was sinless, died for us and rose again.

In this chapter, I have defended the traditional claim that the gospel of salvation, our present spiritual lives and the hope for their fulfilment, do depend upon metaphysical and historical truths. I have held that there is nothing especially strange in this view; and that its rationality is not weakened by the fact that people widely dispute both the facts and the view of salvation we have. I have tried to sketch an explanation of how it can be rational to commit ourselves to faith, even when disputes about it seem to be irresolvable in this life. But there is a special problem about history, and about God's actions in history. What does it mean to say that God acts in history? And how can we tell that he has done so? C says bluntly that there is no evidence of God acting in history at all. If that were true, our understanding of faith and salvation would have to be revised radically. So we must next ask whether it is true.

# 8

## Providence, Prayer and Miracle

Does God act in history? The way this question is formulated may lead us to think of history as a self-contained set of events, running perhaps like clockwork by pre-ordained rules, with every event totally explicable by reference to previous events in history. If God acted here, he would have to interfere in the clockwork; and then we would see that the rules had been disturbed, the laws of nature violated. The acts of God would lie in the area of the odd, the unusual, the arbitrary and irrational. And God himself would be a finite individual waiting outside history, ready to interfere with it from time to time.

But the orthodox doctrine of God is that he is the one and only creator of all things, sustaining them at every moment of their beings by his power. He is not one finite individual among others; he *is* an individual, logically speaking (he is one God, distinguishable from other things); but other realities do not exclude him; they are included in his infinite reality. To say there is a God is to say that ultimate reality is personal. So to say that God acts is to say that reality expresses the purposes of God. The world does not just run according to mechanistic, purposeless laws. It is consciously directed towards a good end; it realizes a purpose, by its very structure and existence. In a real sense, the whole world is the act of God, the expression of his purpose.

To ask about God's acts in history is to ask how particular parts of the world contribute towards the divine purpose, or how they themselves express it. When we say that a particular human person acts, we mean that a certain physical object moves, and its movements are correctly interpretable in terms of an intention to bring about some end. So, when we say that God acts, we mean that certain events happen, and they are correctly interpretable in terms of an intention to bring about some end. There may be many purposes in nature; that is, many natural or historical events may be purposive. If we can give the end to which they are directed, and correctly see them as purposively directed to that end, then we can say that God has acted in those events, in that piece of history.

The question comes down to this: are there pieces of history, which are purposively directed (not by human agents) to good ends? There certainly may be. The difficulty is that many stretches of history seem to issue only in bad ends—the catalogue of human evil sometimes seems limitless—and others seem to be without any point at all. As C puts it, my little experiences of God's providence 'are comparatively small things to set in the balance against the vast and appalling evils of twentieth-century history'.

There is a slight irony here. That is, if God's acts were to be as evident as C would evidently want them to be, then God would have to be rather like the all-determining tyrant that C does not want him to be. If human freedom and self-determination are values—and I do not doubt that they are—God cannot be adjusting things all the time to correct the mistakes that free, self-determining people make. If he really leaves them free, he must leave them free to take the consequences of their actions, and that means that, if people choose to harm each other, the innocent will suffer as well as the guilty. If I get drunk and then drive my car, I may well kill a group of pedestrians. They will be innocent, but they will suffer because of my free, and culpable, action. The price of having a world of free, interrelated beings, is that the innocent will often suffer, if some choose evil. So the terrible suffering of the Jewish people, and many others, in the twentieth-century is due to the evil willed by the National Socialists in Germany and their sympathizers elsewhere. God does not will it. He wills freedom for human beings, of which this is a very undesirable—and avoidable—consequence. God cannot stop it, however, without revoking the very freedom which C admits to be so important.

But now we have to ask whether God can act anywhere, without infringing human freedom. He can, of course, act in inanimate nature; and we may suppose that he does so, by purposively directing nature to the production of sentient and eventually moral beings. There is no established theory of the natural sciences which rules out that possibility, or which even makes it less probable than it seems to common sense. But can he act in human history? Clearly, if he primarily wills freedom, he can only do so in ways which do not infringe freedom. An act of God may be seen in any sequence of events which is directed to the realization of a good purpose. So we may suppose that God may act to strengthen good acts, and to mitigate or weaken bad acts, though without depriving people of responsibility. He may do this, not only in general, but in the day to day lives of ordinary people. So he may strengthen my resolve if I turn to him in prayer, or enlarge my vision. On the other hand, he may weaken my intellect if I am bent on a course of evil, or blunt my perception.

The important thing is that God must never be predictable or usable in his actions. Then he would become just another feature of the universe, under human control, a sort of psychic force, perhaps, which we could control by prayer and fasting. Some accounts of prayer suggest that God is controllable in that sort of way. But God both leaves human freedom intact and preserves his own sovereign freedom by refusing to act in predictable, usable ways. For this reason a truly personal God must act in hidden or ambiguously interpretable ways. It is true that the whole world expresses the being of God, but the preservation of human and Divine freedom means that his actions, the purposive processes in history, must be inaccessible to human techniques of causal explanation and control.

So we cannot think of God as a particular agent within the world. We cannot think of him as a controllable, predictable causal power. The purposes of God are deeply hidden, and so intertwined with the chains of causality and human freedom that they cannot be clearly disentangled and isolated for inspection. Perhaps the best way to think of God's action is to think of it as his presence, drawing things towards himself, guiding or shaping or influencing by the inherent attraction of his own being, attracting things towards their true good. This idea basically comes from Aristotle, who saw the First Cause as drawing things into their proper forms by love or desire. But Aristotle's God was, apparently, quite unchanging and unresponsive to the independently existing world of matter. It was only matter which changed; God, in his changeless perfection, remained unmoved, without even knowledge of the material world which desired him. The Christian God is, however, totally responsive to all that happens, and when he guides things to realize their proper values, he modifies his own being to respond appropriately to creatures. So

95

God's knowledge changes, as the world changes; and his persuasive power adapts to particular circumstances. While his causal influence is constant, a continual pressure towards goodness, the ways in which it is exercised vary in accordance with differing situations.

The Christian must believe, then, that God is active everywhere, even in places of war and disaster, but his action is limited by the nature of the world he has made—a world of general laws and immanent energies—and by the acts of free creatures. Thus it is often impossible to see the realization of good purposes in the course of events. We live in an emergent universe, drawn from nothing, through the abyss of freedom, to a sharing in the divine life of eternity. In places, the picture we see will be very dark; it can even come to seem purposeless. The cry of Christ on the cross, 'My God, my God, why have you forsaken me?' is an authentic cry of dereliction from a world where goodness seems defeated. Even here—and especially here, in fact—God is not absent; his providence is working to bring this terrible evil to good; not to justify its occurrence, but to use it, once it is brought about by free, evil choices, for good. The resurrection brings salvation to the world. That dereliction was used for a great good. It was made part of a purpose, which could not be perceived at the time.

The Christian will want to say this of the most terrible events, like the Holocaust. It was a terrible thing that it ever happened; God did not will it, but it issued from the freedom he gave to creatures. But it does not escape the action of providence and will be used for good. It is dangerous for us to guess exactly how, or to think that evil is all right, if it will be used for good anyway. We will not know the good until the end of all things; it will, like the resurrection, almost certainly extend beyond earthly death; but somehow God can use even that terrible event for good, in ways we cannot predict or lay down in advance.

What we have to say, then, is not that God interferes from time to time in a self-contained mechanistic universe, but that the universe, in its inner nature, is constantly being persuaded or guided to the realization of purposes of value. God's action is everywhere and immanent in all things, but it will become clearer in some places, where we seem to be able to discern the realization of good. We can speak of God's acts, in a particular sense, when we are thinking of a way in which the divine love is being directed in a particular fashion, in response to a specific set of circumstances, to realize an obviously good and fairly immediate purpose. So we may first of all think of particular experiences in our personal lives, of guiding, enlightenment or fortunate co-incidence, as it seemed, and say that these things were providential. But if we do so, we must remember that God's purposes move over aeons of time and vast tracts of history and that they embrace whole centuries of despair as well as moments of individual happiness. All is within the scope of God's providence, his guiding of all things to good, in a world where freedom can obscure and impair that good, but never finally defeat it.

It is in such a context that we must think of prayer, which C regards as having no causal efficacy. Prayer is part of the exercise of human freedom. It is not an attempt to tell God things he does not know or to get him to do things which he would not have bothered to do, though he could easily have done. If God is always drawing the world towards good, but in ways which respect the limits he has set to nature, the activity of intercessory prayer can be seen as a redrawing of those limits, a power he has put into our hands. We do not know the exact extent of our power; we may indeed pray for things which are impossible. But our love may open up the world a little more to God's love. It is obvious that by our actions we can impede God's purposes or co-operate with them. God's purposes are not set just by divine decree, as if we could not affect them at all. God permits us to modify or affect his purposes in detail. Thus our prayers may modify the forms his pressure towards good takes. If God not only draws the world by a universal impulsion, but also responds to it in detail, then it is reasonable to think that he will respond to our prayers by taking them into account, as factors which guide his guiding of the way things go.

In general, we can expect no direct relationship of prayer to answer; we may not get what we pray for. But the Christian may believe that his prayers are always used by God for good. By God's own ordaining, our prayers can guide his particular responses to creatures, the ways in which he draws towards good. In this sense, prayer has a causal efficacy; our praying makes the world other than it would otherwise have been, and it does so by influencing God or the detailed forms of his responsive guiding of creatures.

I suggest that it is sensible, then, to think of God as acting in history, to think of the world as under the all-embracing influence of the Divine persuasion. I entirely agree with C in his rejection of the all-determining, morally arbitrary tyrant. I wonder how many Christians have seriously held that view? Instead, let us think of God as the cross would lead us to think, as the supremely perfect being who creates the world out of overflowing joy and goodness; who allows it freedom, even at the cost of suffering to himself; and who strives to bring creatures to share in his own joy and goodness, simply by the persuasive power of love. The acts of such a God will not be arbitrary interruptions of a self-contained nature; they will be hidden in the warp and woof of the world itself. But they may be discerned both in providential happenings in individual life, where the conditions of time and circumstance allow for them, and in the general emergence in human history of new and higher levels of moral perception or rational understanding.

The Christian religion, however, proposes something more than this. It proposes that a specific revelation of the nature and purpose of God has been given in one piece of human history, not exclusively, but with full and final and definitive adequacy. This is not only providence, the discernment of God's presence and purpose in the natural; it involves miracle, a discernment of God through a raising of things beyond their natural powers. For the Christian, David Hume's well-known definition of miracle as 'a violation of the laws of nature by a supernatural spirit' is laughably inadequate. To begin with, it presupposes the reductivist mechanism which assumes that the world is a non-purposive, deterministic, self-contained machine. Then, it speaks of miracle as simply a violation of these laws, as though it was an external, fortuitous interruption, without real relevance to natural things themselves: and it wholly misses out any real spiritual dimension. The 'spirit' is only another cause; there is no hint of a morally ennobling or personally disclosive element in the experience, nothing whose discernment requires a response of commitment or an initial attitude of trust and expectancy. There is only the extremely funny fact, and the credulous reaction. For Hume, a miracle is just a very rare sort of causality (or it would be, if such things ever happened).

If we are to understand miracle, we must take our understanding from that paradigm for Christian faith, the founding miracle of faith, the resurrection. I will suggest that seven elements of this occurrence, as it is described in the New Testament, are important for the understanding of miracle. First, natural laws were suspended: the body disappeared; apparently materialized and dematerialized behind locked doors, and so on. Even if we do not think of nature as a closed mechanism, and so if we do allow for such extraordinary events to happen, within the scope of laws of probability, they remain very extraordinary. Their timing shows them to be more than random. Here, objects are being purposively changed in ways, which are not covered by the usual laws governing their behaviour. The natural is being taken beyond its normal ('natural') powers for some higher purpose.

Secondly, the resurrection was only seen by the followers of Jesus, not by the Romans or Pontius Pilate, for example. It was not an indisputable sign, equally available to all. It confirmed wavering belief, but did not compel assent. The special case of Paul's vision of the risen Christ may be construed as the confrontation of a deeply pious man with the reality which he had struggled to evade for so long. The miracle came in different ways, not to those who were expecting it, but to those whose hearts were prepared to receive it. It was recognized by the eye of faith, which its occurrence opened.

Thirdly, the resurrection did not occur in a vacuum — as though the resurrection of Queen Elizabeth might have done just as well. It was the fulfilment of dimly understood prophecies and the completion of a whole tradition of developing revelation in the Old Testament. It was not just a funny fact, but an event, which takes its meaning from its context; and in that context, it has a significance for human life which is unique. Though unusual, to say the least, yet its occurrence has an inner reasonableness which puts the Old Testament in a new light for Christians. By hindsight, it almost comes to seem probable, or at least to be the natural, fore-ordained result of the whole train of revelation to Israel. In that sense, it is not just queer.

Fourthly, the resurrection did not avoid or completely abolish evil and suffering. It came through defeat and death, revealing the strength and fidelity of love, not the force of omnipotence. It does not seem that miracles enable us to avoid suffering, but they might enable us to live through it and even achieve good through it.

Fifthly, the resurrection vindicated the life and self-offering of Jesus. He was shown to be Son of God indeed by that final triumph; without it, he would have been just one more failed prophet. The oddity of views, which deny a real resurrection, is that they propose following one of the world's great failures. But, while the resurrection does not detract at all from the heroic self-commitment of the cross, it enables it to be seen rightly as an expression of a love which will surely be fulfilled. That is, in my view, vital to faith. Faith is, above all, the hope for the fulfilment of good; it is quite different from the stoical fortitude, which accepts despair as the last word.

Sixthly, the resurrection shows in a supernatural way what shall be for all; it makes the future present; the world beyond death visible for a moment in this world. The 'breaking' of law is in fact a 'first fulfilling' of human nature, the foretelling of its future destiny. Here we can see how it is not just an arbitrary going-beyond normal powers. It is a fulfilling of those powers, a prefiguring of the completeness which awaits all creatures. The miracle perfects the natural, by binding it in relation to God.

Seventhly, the resurrection mediates salvation to all, bringing the life of God to men, calling for their response of faith, making it available to all. There is a real discernment of God here: of his nature as self-giving love, of his purpose of bringing men to maturity in Christ, of his presence in human nature and his mastery of death.

Using the paradigm of the resurrection, then, we might think of a miracle, in its full form, as a raising of some object beyond its natural powers, to a fulfilment which lies in relation to God, which evokes faith, mediates God's presence and prefigures future glory. Miracle has nothing to do with a magical avoidance of evil. It has to do with knowledge and love of God, and the revelation of his will. On this understanding, miracles are not neutrally available evidence, which can give credence to a set of propositions declared on authority. They are signs of divine purpose, which need to be interpreted in the context of a wider theological view, and suggest particular specifications of that view.

I think it is clear that, if the resurrection had not really occurred, then all that I have said would not obtain. We could not confidently accept Jesus as the bearer of God's word, or believe that we can be redeemed from death and sin. If this historical event has not happened, Christian faith would be false and irrational. So Christian truth depends upon this event having occurred. If that is so, how can we be sure of our faith, since we can never be sure of the occurrence of such a strange event, so long ago, witnessed by so few? It is this question, more than any other, which drives C and those who agree with him into the odd position that historical facts cannot really be important for Christian faith. The position is odd, because C continues to assume that Jesus is very important; and yet we cannot even be sure that he said or did anything ascribed to him in the Gospels; so if he was consistent, C would have to give up any appeal to Jesus at all.

It is, of course, a fact about history that we can never go back and observe the past for ourselves. Many things are now very important to us, which we cannot now verify. We have to rely upon evidence: writings, photographs, archaeological findings, and so on. What evidence have we for the life and teachings of Jesus? It is always possible for a historian to say that the evidence is loaded in some way or is insufficient. It could be argued, on purely historical grounds (though not very plausibly) that Jesus never even existed. We do not expect historians to agree among themselves; so where can we get if we leave the matter to them?

We do not approach the question of Jesus' existence as quite disinterested historians (if there is any such thing). We approach it with an attitude to religion already formed. If we are fairly sure that there is no God, that the universe is purposeless and mechanistic, then no amount of evidence from a time long ago will convince us otherwise. As C says, 'miracles no more happened then than they do today' (44). He will not allow evidence to count, as he is so sure that miracles just cannot happen (there is no God to make them happen). If, on the other hand, we believe that there is a personal God with purposes for the universe, then we might actually expect to find some signs of that purpose somewhere. That will be a natural expectation; so, if we find claims to discern a special purpose of God in the history of Israel, we will look sympathetically at the claim. Our assessment of past probabilities naturally depends upon our prior expectations, and they depend on our general view of the world.

We first ask the general question, 'Is there a God?'; then we ask whether he could be expected to reveal his nature. My own estimate is that we can rationally decide that there is a God and at least be ready to examine carefully claims that he has revealed his nature. We then have to ask which actual tradition of revelation is most acceptable. Here, we will use moral arguments, which seem to advocate the highest morality; factual arguments, which seem to fit the observed facts better; and rational arguments, which seem most consistent or coherent with other knowledge. In the case of the Christian tradition, we need to ask, on the evidence of the Gospels, whether the teachings of Jesus seem to be those of a profound moral and spiritual teacher. We need to ask whether the claims for Christ can be seen to fulfil intelligibly the Old Testament promises, forming a developing pattern of disclosure of the divine. We need to consider the extraordinary growth of the early Church, founded on the testimony of the apostles to the risen life of Christ, and the new liveliness which it inspired in them. We need to ask whether the experience of God through Christ which the Churches now proclaim seems to be a genuine, transforming relationship to a living God; and, of course, we do need to look at other traditions, not to compare so much as to assess the Christian claim to be the fulfilment and completion of all true religion.

All these are matters of complex personal judgement, but they are also very definitely matters of rational assessment, not mere whim. We may reasonably come to the opinion that the Christian tradition of revelation does indeed make a good claim to be the chosen vehicle of God's self revelation. We will then expect to find in that tradition very definite signs of divine purpose; we will take at least its central truths to be definitive symbols or disclosures of God. It is at this point that we see that the miracle of the resurrection is a central truth of Christianity, and at the same time, that a miracle in this tradition is a supernatural fulfilment, which evokes faith and which is therefore necessarily ambiguous or hidden to the neutral, dispassionate spectator. That is, we see that miracles cannot be used as publicly available evidence. They can never be accepted because there is unambiguous evidence for them; in the nature of the case, there cannot be. The reason for accepting them is that they are central elements in a tradition of revelation, which seems the fullest vehicle of God's revelation. In a theistic universe, it is fairly likely that there will be miracles. No particular miracle can be regarded as likely in itself; they are by definition improbable events. Yet miracles like the resurrection can come to have a certain probability, because they are central to a whole tradition; and, by hindsight, they can be seen to be focal points or fulfilments of the sort one might expect from the God, whom the tradition as a whole reveals.

We can now say that the resurrection, that historical fact, is the foundation of the truth of the Christian revelation. So, if the revelation is true, then the resurrection occurred. But we believe that the resurrection occurred primarily because we believe the revelation as a whole is true, adequate, explanatory and morally and spiritually fruitful. In other words, our Christian faith is not based upon our prior assessment of the truth of the resurrection, or any other miracle. We come first to faith, as a practical and living way of relationship to God. But then, exploring its presuppositions historically as well as metaphysically, we find ourselves committed to the truth of various historical events. We accept the history because of our faith, in very much the same way as we accept a certain metaphysical working out of the nature of God because of our experience of the world as personal. There is nothing inconsistent or irrational in this.

C says, 'Talk about God is talk about human experiences'; and it is true that it is the believer's present religious experience, together with his general views of the nature of the world and his basic evaluative commitments, which leads him to talk about God, and about God's acts in history. But it is false to say that talk about God is *nothing but* talk about human experiences, as though no facts or historical occurrences were relevant. We do want to know that our experiences are genuine and appropriate; and it is only appeal to the facts which can show that. Naturally, we cannot get directly either to historical or metaphysical facts, so as to be theoretically certain of our beliefs. But I have pointed out that theoretical certainty is not required for religious commitment. We must posit the facts in objective uncertainty, as presuppositions of the truth of our basic orientation in the world, an orientation we cannot evade or deny, except at the expense of our integrity as persons.

The Christian faith is that God acts in history, and especially in those supernaturalizing moments when the present is transfigured by the intimation of future glory. The resurrection is one moment of time which discloses both the final end of human life and the true nature of divine love. So it is the focal point of all history, at least until that final 'drawing near' of Christ in glory. It is the supreme revelation of God; and once we accept that, it becomes the basis of a total view of the world and human destiny which can meet every demand of rationality and provide enriched understanding and renewed moral vitality.

# 9

## Evil and Evolution

C presents a view of the universe as mechanistic, morally neutral and purposeless. In sharp contrast, the theist sees the universe as purposively tending towards the realization of value, and as expressive, in varying degrees, of an underlying personal and supremely perfect individual, God. This individual includes the universe in his own reality, though in his actual possession of supreme value, he can be distinguished from the developing and finite elements of the spatio-temporal world. It is misleading to think of God as existing quite outside the universe, as though it exists without his continual sustaining presence to everything in it. It is misleading to think of God as determining everything that happens by his omnipotent power. For God freely brings about this particular universe, because it is good in a distinctive and unique way; and he brings it about as a world in which free creatures can emerge and shape their own destinies in interaction with one another. God holds them in being, and he draws things to himself by the persuasive power of his own perfection, but always within the limits he has set to protect the freedom of creatures. God is omnipotent; and it is the extent of his power that he can even create beings which are able to be self-determining—though he could, if he wished, determine them to do whatever he willed.

The theist cannot agree that the universe is valueless or purposeless and that the whole of existence can be exhaustively and exactly described solely by the concepts of mechanistic physics. But there is very little reason why any sensible person should agree to that. Mechanistic physics has been long outdated by developments in quantum field-theory and relativity-physics; and whatever view of the world will emerge from that extremely complex set of theories, it will not be mechanistic. Moreover, there is no reason to suppose that physics, which deals only with the abstract properties of physical things, should give a complete description of everything. In particular, personal existence seems to be quite outside its scope. It is very plausible to believe that the development of sentient and moral beings from a few very simple and elegant laws shows a supremely efficient purpose; and there is no reason in physics why the universe should not express the purposes of a personal reality just as it expresses the purposes of human persons without flaunting the 'laws of physics'. So there is no reason at all why a 'modern man'—if that is a man who takes physics seriously—should not be a theist. In fact, I have suggested that the very success of physics might lead him to a theistic view: the universe is so rational and mathematically beautiful that it does seem to be the expression of intelligence.

What the theist can agree with C in protesting about is a particular naive and mistaken view of what God is, and how he relates to the world. He is not just another person, interfering from time to time in this universe, answering prayers by direct action, and laying down arbitrary laws which must be obeyed, on pain of endless hell-fire. But it is wholly false to suggest that the orthodox, traditional, idea of God in Christianity has ever been this; it has not. Perhaps it will help us to avoid these mistakes more clearly if we think of God as the personal, moral and valuable depth of the world—a perfectly traditional idea, even though, in these words, it is insufficiently worked out and misleadingly vague. The danger is that we may come to think of God as adjectival to the world, as just one aspect of part of a wider reality, which could not exist without the world. That would not be correct either. God is the whole; he is the infinite, outside whom there is nothing. He does include the world in his being, though he need not have done so. The world could not exist without God; there could not be a purposeless universe, because every possible universe depends wholly on God. God always exists, as the necessary and supremely perfect being. But he can, by free creative choice, bring into being a universe of finite beings, which is then a new, contingent part of his all-embracing reality. The existence of a world does change God, and it is here that the traditional theology is unsatisfactory, since it denies any change in God.

On the traditional view, God is eternal (meaning timeless), immutable and impassable (nothing in the world can cause him to feel differently). This view is, of course, as far removed as possible from the naive anthropomorphism that C caricatures, when speaking of God. But its difficulty is that such a God could not freely do anything, could not be changed by creatures, and so could not respond to them creatively or share in their joys and sorrows. He is too much like the God of Aristotle, who does not even know the finite world; who remains frozen in the timeless contemplation of his own perfection, while the material world gets on as best as it can, without his attention or help. Now that view goes to the opposite extreme from C's all-determining, all too responsive, prying tyrant. One God interferes all the time, and the other never does anything at all. As C puts it, 'God . . . is active in just the same way and to just the same degree at every point in the whole universe' (105). But if so, he never does anything in particular, which makes most religious activities like prayer rather pointless. Characteristically, C then says that what happens is that believers bring in another God, a smaller-scale tribal deity, in effect, who can 'intervene *ad hoc* on the small scale'. So we get two Gods, 'the regular cosmic God and the small-scale, interventionist, personal God', who do not fit at all well together. It is predictable that he should think of the small-scale God as intervening *ad hoc,* as though there was nothing rational about the procedure. However, it is true, perhaps, that some people have adopted the idea of the petty prying tyrant, because they were unable to relate to the official idea of the frozen aristocrat.

An intelligible view of God and a mature spirituality need not to have two silly Gods, but to have one sensible God, who can hold together in his own being these two aspects of necessary immutability and of responsive creativity. It is only in this way that one can see the importance both of the prayer of contemplation, attending to the eternal one hidden in the cloud of unknowing, and of the prayer of intercession and thanksgiving, relating to God as a responsive, creative agent. What we need to say is that God is, to use a phrase of the British philosopher Whitehead, *dipolar*; that is to say, there are two poles or aspects to his being. There is a necessary and changeless aspect: God will always and necessarily be omnipotent, wise and good. His supreme perfection cannot be changed at all; nothing can make him more or less perfect; he is always the most perfect possible being. We might say that it is the general nature of God which is changeless and eternal (in the sense of timeless). In this respect, which is like what Whitehead calls the 'primordial aspect' of God, God is distinct from the world and unchanged by it. For the world is not necessary or eternal or changeless, and it depends wholly on God for its existence. It is quite true that, in his primordial aspect, God never actually does anything except, perhaps, contemplate his own perfection. For really doing something would change him. So, in this aspect, God does not even create the world, much less become incarnate in it or redeem it. If that is all there was to God, it would not be irrelevant, but it would not give rise to anything like the Christian religion as we know it.

The other aspect of God's being is called by Whitehead the 'consequential aspect'. It refers to the respects in which God is a personal creative and responsive agent, a being who changes and freely decides, who is contingent and unpredictable in detail. We might say that, as God's nature is changeless, the particular ways in which this nature is realized in diverse actions form the consequential pole of the divine being. In this aspect, God is still not the tyrant who interferes *ad hoc*. Since he is the personal agent who possesses the eternal nature of God, he must always embody supreme perfection and possess all the divine attributes. He must be always and everywhere active to draw things towards good, but he will respond in particular creative ways to different events that happen, so that his acts will be unpredictable in detail and different in different times and places. They will be clearer or more obvious or seem to be more decisive and significant in some places than in others: obviously, the death of Jesus is much more significant, in its total context, than the movement of Pluto around the sun. So God is not everywhere doing just the same thing; he responds appropriately to circumstances. But his acts are not *ad hoc*: he always will respond in some way, though his purposes are so vast and all-embracing that we can scarcely be expected to predict how.

It is in this aspect that God freely creates the world. There are many possible worlds that God could bring into being. He could, if he is perfectly good, bring into being any world which fulfils the following condition: it must be such that every instance of suffering or evil in it is either a necessary condition or a necessary consequence of some vastly overwhelming good for the creature concerned. There might be some possible worlds which contain no suffering at all. Then there is no problem—of course, God could create them, in order to realize forms of finite goodness, which otherwise would not exist. Even though he is supremely perfect himself, he still cannot contain every possible sort of value. For example, he could not contain the value of achieving some difficult task successfully (nothing is difficult for God), and he could not contain the value of physical love (since he has no body). There can be many values, which God on his own cannot contain or enjoy. So he can quite sensibly create a world which can realize those values; then he can enjoy them too, since he knows everything that happens. More importantly, perhaps, he can create new creatures which can enjoy them and share in his joy, so he increases the amount of value in existence. God's value and enjoyment can be changed and increased by the creation of a good world. That does not change God's supreme perfection; he is always supremely perfect. But it does change the specific sorts and amounts of value he enjoys.

Now we cannot say that God *has* to create any of these good worlds; nor can we say, like Leibniz, that he has to create the best of all possible worlds. As Voltaire pointed out, it is really incredible to say that our universe is the best of all possible worlds. We might use the analogy of people having children. It is, on the whole, a good thing to have children; it increases the amount of joy in the world, and makes us happier, too, if we are lucky. But we are not obliged, even on the strictest view, to have all the children we can. It is really up to us to decide whether to marry and have children at all. So, while it is good to have them, we are not obliged to have them. It is the same with creation. It would be good to create good worlds, but God is not obliged to create any of them. If he does, however, then those worlds will not exist 'outside of' God. In having the completest possible knowledge of them and in being able directly to control any part of them, it is less misleading to say that they will be parts of God, as long as we remember that they are contingent, freely created parts, which God could have done without. Probably talking of God as being 'inside' or 'outside' the world is not really very helpful. But at least we must see that God does not just make a world and then leave it to get on by itself, as a self-contained unit. He has to keep it in being in every part and at every moment by his own presence and power; and he is always acting in responsive, creative ways to bring about good purposes within it.

Now we have just seen that there might be many possible good worlds. God does not have to create any of them; so it does not matter, absolutely, which of them he does create. He does not have to create the best possible. In fact, the idea of a 'best possible' world probably does not make sense. It is rather like speaking of the 'best possible symphony' or the 'best possible painting'. We cannot rank worlds on a simple scale like that; so there will always be many good but quite different worlds that God could make. Which one should he make? He can make any he likes; that is his creative freedom, and it cannot be dictated at all. If he does not make a world, no one in it can complain, since they will not exist. If he does make a good world, whichever it is, everyone in it can only give thanks that they do exist in such a good world, seeing that they could not have existed in any other. So, whichever world God makes, everyone in it will be glad that he chose to make that one—what a happy state of affairs.

The trouble is that our world does not seem to be much like that. The huge amount of suffering in our world is the most powerful argument against there being a good God at all. How could he make this one? We had no problem with saying that God could create any world without suffering in it. But I have mentioned that he could also create worlds with suffering, as long as this suffering was necessary to an overwhelming good. If we think again of all the worlds God could create, we can imagine them being stretched out in a line, from extremely good worlds at one end to extremely bad worlds at the other. Some of these bad worlds will be such that God could not create them; the suffering in them is not necessary to a greater good. There will be a lot of worlds that God cannot create; so we can draw a line at a certain point, and say that God can create any of the worlds above the line, and none of the worlds below the line. Now I think we might well say that our actual world, the one we live in, is one of the very worst worlds God could have created. Still, it is an above-the-line world; so it is a good thing that it was created. If it had not been created, we would not have existed at all; in a better world, we would have no place; we would not be let in. So our world is both one of the worst God could have made and also a good world to have created.

Can we explain this a little further? Let us look again at the general character of our world, seen as purposively orientated towards the realization of some distinctive value, which no other world would have. One of the greatest discoveries of the modern age has been evolution, not just Darwin's account of the emergence of humans from lower species, but the whole conception of the universe as an emergent, evolving system, over millions of years moving from a few simple laws and elementary particles to the complex personal life of free moral agents on earth (and no doubt elsewhere too). As we look at this process, at first sight it seems natural to see it as the expression of an unfeeling mathematician, inexorably moving from inert unconscious matter to the development of mind and self-awareness. The individual seems relatively unimportant in this scheme; whole species become extinct. Yet the process as a whole goes on, so that self-aware consciousness is the emergent character of the universe. So we might see the world as the self-expression of Reason, limited perhaps by the necessities of the matter from which it begins, moving towards the goal of complete self-knowledge, using and discarding individuals in its own self-unfolding process.

That is a plausible view; it is, in essence, the view held by the philosopher Hegel; and I think it represents the state of modern knowledge better than C's rather quaintly old-fashioned Positivism. It is not quite the theistic view, however; I mention it because it is plausible, and offers an illuminating perspective on theism, which helps to correct its more anthropomorphic mistakes. Of particular interest is the stress on emergence, on the development of new qualities over time (a fact which Hegel lived too early to appreciate fully). This is a universe which generates out of itself its own creatively emergent future. That is not a matter of pure chance; the direction is built into the structure of things from the first; and, for the theist, things are drawn towards new creative actualizations by the attraction of the ideal, the supreme perfection, God. To use an old analogy, God is like the sun, drawing out plants from the earth to flower and blossom in its light. The analogy is, of course, inadequate; for the power of the sun is impersonal, unconscious and quite general, whereas the influence of God is personal, conscious and particular. He apprehends and responds to particular events as they are, and modifies his persuasive influence to guide them in appropriate and particular ways. Nevertheless, it may be a helpful image to think of the universe as drawn from the earth—from the general, indeterminate, non-individual and inert realm of brute matter— towards particular and determinate beauty, increasing individuality and awareness, by the power of supreme perfection. We are not to think of the universe as pushed on its way down predetermined tracks by a God who then goes to sleep until things go wrong. We are rather to think of individual forms as emerging from inert matter, drawn out by the ever-present responsive guiding of supreme beauty.

At early and simple levels — in the vastnesses of cosmic space — there is virtually no scope for free response or individuality, no consciousness or risk of failure. The world is governed by a structure of elegant form, but it is completely general. Nevertheless even there, certain elements must exist as the basis for further evolution. There must be a structure of general law; otherwise there would be no predictable, firm base for the development of more complex structures later on. There must also be an element of actual or potential randomness or indeterminacy, as the foundation for future freedom and individuality of response to the drawing Ideal. If everything was determined, freedom could never come to exist. So, while indeterminacy is certainly not enough for freedom, it is a necessary condition of it. Physicists do seem to find such indeterminacy in nature; though it cancels out at the macro-atomic level, where there are no other influences which might utilize its possibilities. Finally, there must be the potential for emergence; that is, the universe must contain in itself the potentiality for later conscious self-shaping. Life or consciousness will not need to be externally imposed; they will arise from the inherent finality of matter, as it gradually realizes its own emergent properties by increasingly complex interactions. Generality, indeterminacy and emergence are three basic properties of our universe. They are essential to the coming into being of the sort of human life we have. Human beings are animals, moral consciousnesses which have evolved from simpler, inanimate objects, and which still carry much of their past with them, even while evolving towards a creative future.

By the time we arrive at human life, we have conscious beings which are to some extent self-shaping. The human race is now beginning to hold its future in its own hands. But in order to do this, it still depends upon those basic properties of the universe which make its distinctive way of being possible. However much in control of his destiny man is, he remains an essentially dependent being, not in an offensive, limiting way, but in that he obviously cannot control the continuing existence of the basic laws of the universe, which he uses to control the future. The freedom which C so rightly stresses is, at the same time, limited by the necessities of the world; so there must always be a proper and inevitable form of dependence as well as of autonomy. So humans rely on the generality of natural laws in order to predict and manipulate and understand the world. They rely on the indeterminacy in the world, to realize new, free and creative modes of action and expression. They rely, too, on the continuity of emergence to provide them with that basic animal and social nature which they can now consciously begin to shape in accordance with their perception of ideals. The inanimate world is naturally quite unconscious of God's shaping, guiding power, drawing it on towards consciousness, knowledge and freedom. Human beings can become aware of this divine energy, though they may seem to perceive it in the form of ideals, rather than of an existent perfection to which they are called to make a creative response.

It may be held that traditional religion has been backward-looking rather than forward-looking, conformist rather than creative, preferring a static body of authoritative doctrine to the free pursuit of new knowledge and critical reflection. I doubt if one can accuse the Christian faith, as such, of these things, but they are characteristics of certain forms of religious life, the forms against which Marx protested so effectively. There are reasons why religion should look to the past. If God has acted in self-revealing ways, then it is important that we should remember those ways and seek to make them effective in our own lives. But if one sees that God is still acting in the present (and the Christian doctrine of the Spirit helps us to see this); and if one sees how much religious beliefs have changed and developed over the centuries; then one becomes aware that we cannot be simply bound to repeat the past. Indeed, a central part of the Jewish and Christian traditions is forward-looking: it looks for the coming of God's Kingdom, for the drawing-near of Christ, in a cosmic manifestation. As Paul himself puts it, the faith is not bound by written words from the past, but by the living presence of the Spirit of the risen Christ, the one who is to come, whose full understanding lies in the future. So we should see God as having, indeed, shown himself in history, in the life of Christ, by that miraculous act manifested in a human life. But that very act throws us forward, to live towards the future, not a future of death, but of hope for renewal and fulfilment. The God who has shown himself in Christ draws us on to a future fulfilment of his

Kingdom. Perception of this God leads us to be critical of all established institutions and systematized formulations of belief. Christ proved to be too hard for the religious institutions of the Judaism of his day to contain. So he cannot be contained by any religious institution which threatens to put itself, its own status, power or formulations of belief, in place of God's Spirit, to demand the obedience due only to him. But though whole churches may defect, as human institutions, the Church itself, the hidden body of Christ, will always contain the power of its own renewal. If we, as members of the Church, protest about its unthinking conformism, then we contribute, in our way, to that renewal.

God shows us, in Christ, the form of the future; and that is where we should be looking. That future will be built upon human effort and invention. But such effort, where it is rightly directed, will be in response to the leading of God, the divine lure of perfection built into the heart of our world. We might say that the human race has passed through its childhood, when it viewed itself as bounded by arbitrary supernatural powers, obeying the commands of God, helpless before powers it could not understand or control, and having no idea of a developing past or future, but living the daily repetitive cycle of seasons and simple joy and hardship in the light of religious tradition. At first, the invention of writing only reinforced the power of tradition, since it enabled traditions to be passed on reliably from one generation to the next. Yet it was revolutionary in its ultimate effect; since it enabled information to be accumulated and disseminated, which was eventually bound to undermine all claims to finality in the first texts.

With the beginning of technology, and the discovery for the first time of real power over nature, man came to adolescence. With all the rebellion of the adolescent, he threw over the authority of any external God, revelled in his own autonomy and regarded tradition as no more than superstition. I hazard the suggestion that, when man comes to maturity, he will be able to come to terms with God in a less purely authoritarian and more interactive way. He will not be confined by traditional rules, which seem, after due reflection, to be irrational or harmful. But he will not claim absolute autonomy either. Seeing that the tyrant God was a projection of his own fear, he can begin to apprehend the God of love as the environing reality to which he responds in his own unique and creative way. So religion will not be a force of traditionalist reaction (though it will always value tradition) but a resource for vision and inspiration, for carrying a vision of the future and conveying a guiding, strengthening, illumining power, which can help us achieve that vision by our own self-shaping. We cannot yet tell what the religion of the future will be like; it might be very different from the institutions of our own day, but the Christian will believe that the self-revealing of God in the past, and especially in Jesus Christ, will find its true completion in that future and that he will be able to recognize Christ truly and fully in that community living under the guidance of God.

The picture that I have tried to present is that of human life as standing at a pivotal point in the evolution from matter towards a community of Spirit, in which free self-conscious agents can creatively co-operate in a society irradiated by the unifying power of supreme love, a love which has been the driving-force of evolution throughout. The distinctive value of this particular world is that it represents the positing by a supremely perfect being of something at almost the opposite pole of reality from itself. Whereas God is conscious, perfect, individual and active to a supreme degree, matter is unconscious, value-neutral, indeterminate and inert. Yet God is able to transform this obverse projection of himself into a world which expresses his own perfections in finite and appropriate ways. Hegel saw this process as necessary to God; for him, the being of God lay essentially in the process of objectification into the opposite and reconciliation or transformation of that into perfection. Most Christians have not accepted the idea that God has to create this world and that it is a necessary phase of his own self-manifestation. Indeed, such a stress on necessity threatens to undermine contingency, real individuality, freedom and moral value in creatures, by making them all parts of one necessary self-realizing process.

Nevertheless, we can say that the possibility of this world clearly lies in God; and the sorts of values which such an objectified and reconciled world can realize will be quite distinctive and unable to exist in any other sort of world. If we add to Hegel's picture a firmer stress on the importance of individual effort, so that creatures really do have responsibility for what happens, so that the world is unpredictable in detail and so that moral value can be lost as well as won, then we have something we could call a meaningful Christian world-view that seems to fit the facts as we know them today, and to preserve the essential Christian doctrines too. So God creates a world with properties very unlike his own. He makes it possible for beings to arise in this world, which come to have responsibility for their own lives and the future of their world. He makes creaturely freedom possible, but posits as the ultimate goal a community of persons, living in freely accepted relation to him. As this world develops, God's own experience changes and he is himself involved in creative response to the world. But the whole thing is not just an exercise in extending God's awareness, as though it was a divine day-dream. It is, just as importantly, the real bringing into existence of creatures which feel and act and know and which have a responsibility for the continuing evolution of the world.

But if this world contains distinctive goods, which could not exist in any other world, and which are intrinsically worth having, it will also contain great evils, and the possibility of even greater evils. Where there are general laws, particular accidents to sentient beings which are governed by those laws are unavoidable. Earthquakes, typhoons and floods follow from general laws of nature, but are very unfortunate for any animals which get in the way. Where there is indeterminacy, accidents are bound to occur. In the same way, where there is emergence, there is the risk of failure as well as success and of evolutionary dead-end and retrogression. So much natural evil is a necessary condition of having a world in which developing beings have freedom.

Furthermore, where beings are free to help one another, they are also free to harm one another. In such a world, the innocent will often suffer. All the wars and brutalities so apparent in our century, but always existing in the world, are necessary consequences of the misuse of freedom. They are unfortunate, and are certainly not willed by God; but he cannot prohibit them, if freedom is to remain.

In general, then, we can say that this world is one which contains distinctive goods; and in which the many evils are either necessary conditions or consequences of the existence of those goods. It looks as if this world is (just?) creatable by a perfect being. There are two considerations suggested by Christian faith which strengthen this rather tentative conclusion (it is tentative, because we do not *know* that these evils are necessary to the goods; but we can see that they may be). The first is belief in life after death, which is entailed by the fact of the resurrection; the second is belief that God shares in our suffering, which is entailed by the fact of the crucifixion.

If we believe in life after death, then we can say that every creature will have the opportunity of a literally endless joy; and, that joy will in some way take into account and use the suffering that has been endured on earth. In other words, the suffering will not be wholly useless; it can be made part of subsequent experience in a positive way. Now I think that if any person, however much he now suffers, were assured of such an endless joy afterwards (and if he could see how his suffering was a necessary consequence of the possession of freedom by creatures), he would agree that it was worth his being created, since he would not have existed at all without the suffering. If this dark world is in fact a preliminary to an utterly overwhelming good, that increases the justifiability of its creation immeasurably. It is not really that we want compensation for our sufferings now. The point is that there must be a very good reason for all the suffering in a world created by God. The strongest reason of all would be that the suffering is part of a world, whose general nature is necessary to the fulfilment of an overwhelming good. The hiddenness of God is a condition of freedom; the occurrence of suffering is a consequence of freedom. But the value of freedom depends upon it having a positive outcome, and that is only possible, for most people, beyond death. So it is my conclusion that life after death is a fact, if this world is indeed created by a perfect God, and that it does fully justify the existence of this world; not just as an external consolation prize, but as the realm where persons can find their proper fulfilment.

However, the suffering does exist, and is a terrible thing with which to have to cope. One of the greatest and indeed unique teachings of the Christian faith is that God shares in our sufferings. He does not stand apart and observe them from afar; he enters fully into the world he has made and himself suffers the worst consequences of free creation. One might have thought that C would approve of the idea of a suffering God, as at least it is far removed from the power-mad tyrant, whom he dislikes so much. But he does not like this idea either. If a perfect God exists, he says, then 'we deny that moral evil and tragedy are anything more than superficial' (112). This is apparently because he assumes that a perfect God cannot create a world in which there is tragedy and evil. I think I have sufficiently dealt with that point. The theist does not have to deny that evil exists and is a terrible thing. He is not offering a facile solution, and saying, 'Everything will be all right; don't worry'. Often silence is the only realistic answer to great suffering. For the suffering has to be *endured*; no intellectual argument is going to ease it. Like Job, the man in agony does not want intellectual arguments; he wants sympathy and some resource of strength to help him endure. He has to give meaning *to* his suffering; and he cannot do that by being told that it will eventually go away.

What is wrong with these facile optimistic solutions is that one cannot say that everything will be all right, *whatever* your attitude to your suffering. You have to seek for faith, patience and hope and you have to endure a great deal of breaking-down of previous expectations and desires. But, while a facile solution cannot be given, it is *very* important to give hope; and that is done by personal presence and by trying to make the presence of God known. Suffering is terrible, but God is present in it; meaning can be found in and through it; in real desolation there can be a breaking-down of self, which can be a new beginning. Jesus' cry from the cross is the paradigm of the actual Christian approach to the sufferer. It is facile to say, 'You will be resurrected tomorrow'; the agony is too real. But if faith in a present, sharing and suffering God is justified, then he will raise us to fulness of life; and it is necessary to believe that, if not to say it, if belief in a perfect creator is to remain.

What is wrong with the suffering God, then, the God who gives meaning to agony by his presence and sharing? For C, such a God is too anthropomorphic; he is not 'religiously adequate'. For, experiencing conflict and affliction himself, he fails to achieve the idea of perfection, and still 'struggles to achieve salvation'; he is still 'in need of deliverance and victory over evil as we are' (112); so he cannot assure us of permanent victory and salvation. It is rather odd that C should say this, since he does not believe in the possibility of full salvation for anyone—it is too idealistic altogether. But at least he wants God to be a perfect ideal, even though he has no actual existence. A suffering God, he implies, could not be such an ideal.

But is this true? It is a very Platonic notion of perfection, that a perfect being must be supremely happy, and can never change in any respect at all, since then, he would either get less happy, or become happier than he was, which would show that he was not perfect at first. Both these are unacceptable for Plato, but if we forget Plato for a moment and ask what properties we think a perfect being would have, surely a capacity to be freely creative— to be, in C's term, 'autonomous'— and so a capacity to change, would be included. As I have pointed out, God's *nature* is immutable; he is always the most perfect being there is; and he is always the most perfect being possible at any moment. But he changes in his actions; and if that means that he continually has new experiences, then in a sense he does have more good things at a later moment than at an earlier one. The fact that God in this sense always gets better, does not mean that his nature changes or that he becomes morally better; it does not mean that he was not always the most perfect being possible at every moment. The Christian God, unlike the God of Plato and Aristotle, is temporal; and that is more perfect than being immutable in every aspect, because it enables him to be creative.

Furthermore, once such a being had created a world with suffering in it, it is surely more perfect to sympathize with and share in that suffering than to remain indifferent to it. The idea of a God who suffers is religiously adequate; and does not entail the idea that God is in need of salvation. He remains omnipotent, and his suffering is included within a wider joy that we can scarcely conceive. It is by his free choice that he suffers, and there is no possibility at all that evil may conquer him. He does not struggle against evil, as a finite, struggling being. Remaining omnipotent, he freely chooses to share in our suffering, precisely so that he can help us, not by force, but by sympathy and the persuasion of love. The idea of perfection is not, after all, the idea of a pure and quite self-sufficient happiness, untouched by anything that might happen in the world. It is the idea of a personal being which responds in the fullest way to all finite experiences, including them within his own being, and working creatively to weave them into a whole of unique value. The final success of his creative enterprise is assured by his omnipotence. The freedom of creatures is guarded by his non-coercive love. The pain of creatures is transfigured by his embracing care and wisdom. This is not a static impassive joy, the eternal Narcissist in a world of pain. It is the full responsiveness of the supremely perfect being in a world of creatures which it wishes to share in his infinite delight in all values. It is the joy of the supreme lover who gives himself to his beloved, to draw the beloved into the enriched perfection of his own being.

Once we see that God is a being of supreme power and love—the triumph of his love made certain by his power; his power exercised only through the persuasion of love—then we see that the image of the cross and resurrection exactly conveys the true picture of God. The God revealed in Christ should never be pictured as a tyrant or as a helpless fellow-sufferer; he is one whose love is stronger than death. His objective existence is something which does not stifle human existence, but which gives meaning and hope in a world, which has been darkened by sin and ignorance. Men are called into being by love, not only to commit themselves to the way of self-sacrificial love, but to find their true fulfilment in the being who is, not self-sufficient power and happiness, but self-giving creativity and love.

# 10

## Immortality

One of the main reasons for the development of radical forms of Christian theology is the loss of belief in life after death. Once that has gone, the existence of suffering is impossible to reconcile with the traditional belief in the objective existence of a perfectly good God. So it becomes natural to reinterpret theistic belief in terms of a purely moral or attitudinal commitment. I have argued, however, that such commitment cannot be justified or shown to be rational unless it does presuppose an objective God. And the claim that it needs no justification deprives it of significance, in a world where people are trying to ensure that their beliefs are reasonable. So it is that the belief in a good God, whose nature is primarily that of creative, redemptive love—the love shown in Christ—entails belief in life after death. The Christian who believes that he experiences the presence of such a God in his life will be bound to hope for the fulfilment of the divine promises for the whole world. A Christian is committed to belief in immortality, for two main reasons: the existence of a God of love and the resurrection of Jesus. The whole life of faith is one of trusting that the love which we fitfully apprehend in this life will be clearly seen hereafter.

This belief is quite basic to Christianity, but it is widely denied; and it is that denial, which has made the problem of suffering seem so much greater in our century than it has ever seemed before, even though there has always been vast suffering in the world. It is denied, because it is held that human personality is essentially dependent on the physical body and so could not survive death. C adds to this an argument that people are so much products of their time and culture that they could not be the same people outside it; we cannot be the same people in a very different time and place. Some attempt must therefore be made to show how I could survive the death of my body.

Let me say at the outset that one great drawback in this area is simply lack of imagination. If we cannot imagine what it is like to live in very different circumstances, we may be tempted to say that it is actually impossible to do so. But such allegations of impossibility have had a very bad time in the past. People said that it was impossible to travel to the moon; impossible to speak to others over vast distances, impossible for objects to act on each other at a distance (even Newton felt that); and impossible to travel faster than sound. It is very difficult indeed to show that something is actually impossible; and I do not really see how anyone can prove that immortality is impossible, even if we cannot imagine what it will be like. But I want to go further, and say that we can imagine what it could be like. I want to extend the imagination quite a way, until we see how we could live without our physical bodies. Some of the ways I must use, to help us to extend our imaginations, will seem very odd. But the whole point is just to show that certain things are imaginable. Although I do not actually know what life after death is like, if we can even imagine a possible life after death, then we know that it really is possible. At the end, I will give another reason for thinking that there actually is such a life, in addition to the two already mentioned, which are the main ones for a Christian.

First of all, then, remember how much our bodies change during our lifetimes. From being very small babies, we may become big and strong, only to become wizened, toothless and bent in old age. No one doubts that I remain the same person through all these changes, but what makes the baby the same person as the old man? The answer might be that there is a spatio-temporal continuity traceable between the two. The body moves through a continuous path in space and time, without any gaps, and the changes which it undergoes are very gradual, not sudden huge jumps. But now, suppose the world is slightly different; suppose we visit a planet in a far galaxy where people disappear completely for short periods. Then they reappear just as they would have been at the next moment, if they had continued in existence as we do. Surely the existence of these temporal gaps would not make us call them different people. We would just say that, on this planet, people occasionally disappeared, perhaps under regular and stateable conditions (when the third sun eclipsed one of the others), and reappeared when the eclipse was over. If this happened to everyone on the planet, it would seem quite normal. Now if we ask how long such a temporal gap could be, I think we must say that it does not matter, unless the world changed so much in the meanwhile that people no longer knew where they were or what to do, when they reappeared. The gap could very easily be a few days or weeks, at any rate. When, in a popular TV series, the crew of a space-ship 'beam down' to a planet, they do cease to exist in one place and appear in another after a temporal gap, and we have no trouble in recognizing who they are.

There could be a problem here, of course. In one episode, when a person disappeared in one place, two exactly similar persons appeared in another. Which, you might ask, is the real person? The philosopher Bernard Williams has argued that since no person can be in two places at one time, neither of the two appearing persons can be the same person. And, since there is no way to prefer one to the other, neither of them can really be the same as the person who was beamed down. It follows from his argument, of course, that any future resurrection for human beings is impossible, for the resurrected people would not really be the same as us, at all. But I do not think we would say this. A much more likely thing to say is that one person has become two. From the point at which two of them appear on the planet's surface, they are two different though very closely similar people, just like identical twins, or people cloned from the same cell. But they both used to be the same person. It is true that no person can be in two places at the same time, but one person can become two. So, obviously, both would be held responsible for whatever had been done by their previous common self, but they will from now on be treated as separately responsible. Of course, we can presume that God will not, at the resurrection, create two of everybody, but he could cause the dead to appear again on earth, as they had been at the moment of death; and if he did, then they would be recognizably the same people. The mere existence of a temporal and spatial gap would not matter.

That, however, is not what happens at the resurrection, at least according to Christian belief. It would be a bit sad if we were mostly resurrected wizened and toothless. We would prefer to be resurrected in a nice new healthy body, not too fat or too thin, not too old or too young. Could this be arranged? Well, let us press our imagination a little further. Let us ask how much it is possible for a body to change. From baby to old man is a large change, but could one, on yet another amazing and faraway planet, change gradually into a completely different shape—say, for the purpose of argument, a parrot (a very large, intelligent parrot)? We are familiar with changes just as drastic, in nature, from tadpole to frog, caterpillar to butterfly. Could humanoids not change their form in a similar way? I do not see why not. Now you might say that it is again continuity which is important, the gradualness of change. But why? The difficulty is, perhaps, the lack of causal explanation for such sudden changes. But if it was a causal law, on this planet, that everyone changed from human form into parrot-form (while retaining the same memories, hopes, aims, likes and dislikes) at the age of thirty, we would surely come to accept that as normal. Obviously, some of our desires and hopes would have to change. It would be odd to find a parrot who likes beer as much as I do, but not impossible. The hopes and desires which would have to change would be those which are directly physical, like sexual attraction, but we would get used to that.

Now we can put these two things together, and suppose that, at the age of thirty, everyone disappears. They then reappear some time later, as huge intelligent parrots, in another part of the world. I submit that, despite this great change and this spatio-temporal gap, we would all agree that the humanoid and the parrot bodies were the same person, at least if it happened to everyone, and there was some causal explanation of the change (we could apply to the usual mad scientist with a teleporter to help us out).

Now I have not invented this story just for fun. I want to establish that persons could remain identifiably the same, even if they had quite different sorts of bodies, in a different place and at a different time. To help our imaginations even more, think of the very strange experience, common to almost all of us, of dreaming. Sometimes I seem to see myself in my dreams, and to be quite sure that it is me, walking around. But that 'me' obviously does not have a physical body and is not walking around in ordinary public space and time at all, for my body is lying in bed. Some people have thought that in dreams I do walk around in a different and strange world. Whether or not that is true, all I want to suggest is that we do have, in fact, a fairly good idea of what it would be like to exist in a different (though in some ways similar) body, in a different space and time from the one in which we walk around during the day.

It is not without interest that the experiences of people who have been clinically dead, but have come back to life; of spiritualists who claim to have some contact with the dead; and of various religious seers, all bear very great similarities to this dream-state. People, who have 'died' clinically, often speak of moving through a tunnel towards a place of light; of hovering above their physical bodies and observing what is going on around them from outside those bodies; and of meeting recognized friends. There is a disconnection with this physical body and yet the friends do have recognizably similar bodies, while not being in this space-time. There are, in other words, experiences bearing a close similarity to human sense-experiences, even though there are no longer any bodily senses functioning. There is spatial movement, physical form and some sort of bodily existence, though it is not in this space-time. The analogy with dreams is close enough for us to call this first stage of after-death experience the 'dream-state', *kama-loka* in Indian philosophy.

The point of my imaginary examples was to help us see that we could continue to exist as the same people, even in a different space-time from this one, and in a body which was different in significant ways from these physical bodies. Now suppose that at death we do pass into a dream-world. Since this would happen to everyone, it would be quite normal. We even have intimations of it in our own dreams, but it seems unusual or queer to us, because we have come to associate ourselves too closely with these gross physical bodies which we now have. There would be a causal explanation for it. Ultimately, the cause would be God, but no doubt there are laws of spiritual/physical interaction as yet unknown to us. We would have bodies which bore some similarity to those we had on earth, but without many of the defects: we might grow new teeth and less wrinkles. But we would probably not be parrots; we would be humanoid, in a transformed, renewed way. We might say that our bodies would more directly express our real personalities; and perhaps they would be much more under our mental control, so that we could make them change, fade or solidify, just as they do, in an uncontrolled way, in dreams.

This dream-world would be in time and would contain spatial relations (just as our dreams do); things would be spatially related to one another; and—here the world is unlike our dreams—this space would not be private to us, a space for our own imaginings and fantastic day or night dreams. It would have a kind of public character; it would be shared between many beings; there would be real relations between people in it. Again, it might be rather different from this space in which we now live. As the philosopher Henry Price put it, it might be ideo-plastic; that is, it would be much more under the control of the mind, more shapable by ideas. We could move by teleportation, appear and disappear and make ourselves known to others or not. So, while there could be a fairly stable set of relationships in this world, within which different people could exist, the forms of their existence and appearance to one another could change and be under conscious control much more than they are now.

I certainly do not believe in the resurrection because of some such theory of the after-life as this, but, if this account or something rather like it, is true, it does give the most plausible account I know of the resurrection of Jesus. Jesus appeared after his death, in very unusual ways. He walked to Emmaus for some miles, without being recognized, until he chose to reveal himself. He could pass through closed doors, though he could also eat. He could appear and disappear; and he eventually disappeared in a cloud. C would dismiss all these accounts as legends and he complains that a revived corpse simply could not do all these odd things. But the whole point is that the resurrection body is not a 'revived corpse'. As Paul put it, 'Flesh and blood cannot inherit the Kingdom'. The body of Jesus disappeared; it was not revived as an ordinary physical object. It was transformed completely into something quite different, into the glorious body of the resurrection world. On this account, Jesus was not really unique in living in bodily form after death; everyone does that. Everyone passes into the dream-world and has a 'spiritual' ideo-plastic body, a body fully expressive of the personality which it incarnates. Jesus was unique in being able to reveal this spiritual body to his followers and to assure them that the gulf between life and after-life was bridged, so as to vindicate his own life of obedience to the Father. By his appearing, Jesus showed his triumph over the powers of evil, and when he returned to 'sit at God's right hand', his spiritualized body passed for ever back into the after-world, to express there the incarnate love of the creator of all.

This is not the place to speak in detail of biblical views of immortality, but the classical text is Cor. 15, and a look at that chapter shows that, when this physical body dies, we shall have a different, spiritual body. 'If Christ is preached as raised from the dead, how can some of you say that there is no resurrection of the dead?' (12). There is a resurrection, not just a disembodied survival of the soul without any body at all. It was Plato and Descartes who talked of the survival of a completely disembodied soul; the Christian doctrine has always been of the resurrection of the body.

Since Paul talks of the dead as having 'fallen asleep', he presumably does not think that the resurrection follows immediately upon death. He probably thinks of everyone being resurrected at the return of Christ in glory; in the letters to the Thessalonians, this impression is given. On the other hand, Jesus talks of God as being the 'God of the living, not of the dead'; and when the Roman Catholic Church declared the Assumption of Mary, it implicitly declared that the dead are already resurrected to eternal life.

In any case, it is wholly mistaken to think that the resurrection of the body is the resuscitation of our corpses. 'What you sow is not the body which is to be', writes Paul (37). The resurrection body will be imperishable, glorious and powerful: 'It is sown a physical body, it is raised a spiritual body' (44). At the Last Judgement, 'we shall all be changed . . . for this perishable nature must put on the imperishable' (53). So his doctrine is quite clear, that the resurrection body is a quite different, spiritual body; not the one in which we die, though having a relation to our physical body, the relation, he says, of seed to full-grown plant. It is not a case of humans turning into parrots. It is more that a decaying, fragile, weak body will be transformed into a strong, imperishable body, fully expressive of our personalities and fully under their control. It is clear that this is what Paul took the resurrection body of Jesus to be and that this is the pattern of our own immortality.

It is undoubtedly true that talk of the Last Things, of death, judgement, heaven and hell, in the New Testament is richly metaphorical. Talk of Jesus sitting at the right hand of God and of him returning on the clouds with the sound of a trumpet, is poetry rather than a literal description of anything. These phrases express truths in metaphorical terms and spiritual realities in physical terms. But what they express is not just an inner spiritual state or commitment. It is something about the ultimate nature of the world, which cannot be more straightforwardly expressed in terms available to the culture in which they were written, or perhaps in any terms available to us now. The imagery is physical and immediate: Jesus sits at God's right hand until, quite soon, he will rise to return on the clouds; the dead, in their transfigured forms, would come with him; and those living at that time would also be transformed and rise to meet him in the air. Then there would be a great and terrible time of judgement, a messianic reign, and at last a new heaven and a new earth. All this has been a rich source of mad theories and eccentric ideas, as people have tried to interpret literally what was symbol and metaphor. I think that it is wiser not to try to translate the symbols into factual details, but to grasp the basic underlying ideas. These are, I suggest, that Jesus has triumphed over death and evil; that the future consummation of human development will lie in a discovery of and union with the cosmic Christ; that the dead will be transfigured by union with him; and that suffering and evil will continue, until in the end they are finally conquered by love. In other words, we must not take any of the symbols to be direct, literal statements of the truth (just as we must not take the narrative of the creation story in Gen. 1 to be a literal history of the first week of the world's existence). The symbols express important truths, which must be interpreted in the light of the basic revelation in the person of Jesus himself. God will triumph; this triumph has been prefigured and assured in Christ; the dead can find fulfilment; these are the great truths underlying the New Testament imagery.

I would not claim that the New Testament gives a literal and accurate picture of the after-life, but it does express the truth that there is an after-life; that in it human personality will be more fully expressible, not changed out of recognition; and that the basic model for it must be the resurrection, the glorified body, of Jesus. If we look at the way the idea of 'salvation' developed throughout the whole Bible, I think we can say that the idea is communal; it is not individuals, who are saved in isolation; it is communities who are saved. It is historical, at least in the sense that it must offer an intelligible development of the sort of lives we live now; so that what we do now is important to what happens in the 'saved' society. Again, then, we may suppose that the after-life must offer the possibility of communal development of the same personalities as we are now developing. So, remembering Paul's warning, in 1 Cor. 15, that we do not know what sort of bodies we shall actually have, it seems right to suppose that we will possess bodily existence in a space-time with slightly, but not completely, different, properties from those of our present space-time.

Some people think that a bodily existence that continued for ever would be rather boring. If you think of it as a continual playing of harps and singing of hymns, it would be, for most of us. But that is because we are so conscious of the passing of time that we quickly come to think of activities as boring. Think, however, of the most intensely satisfying experience that you have ever had; and, for those lucky enough to have it, this will almost always be an experience of intense personal love. At such times, usually for rather short periods, everything takes on a new beauty; we do not notice time passing; we can revel in the present moment as wholly satisfying; we forget our worries and anxieties and do not think about what will happen tomorrow. Now Christians speak of heaven as being in love with God, the being of infinite value. We may suppose that, if we are truly and fully in love with him (because he fills us with his love, and we gladly allow him to do so), we will not notice the passing of time; but every moment will be transfigured and joyful. Boredom will not be an option. Only hell is boring, for there we are unable to accept and be taken into God's love.

Could this love become so complete that we pass into timelessness? I simply do not think we can say what the ultimate destiny of the human soul is. It is enough to think of the next stage, and to know that it is a growing into God. But, since we have got used to stretching our imaginations, let us attempt one further journey of imagination, this time to show how the mind, spirit or soul can continue without any body. For we might see, in the independence of spirit, and in its own inner purposiveness, a reason for thinking that life after bodily death would at least be a very natural possibility, not just a peculiar anomaly in a materialistic universe.

What is a body? First, it is a limited area of space, over which we have, to a certain extent, direct causal control, that is, we can raise our arms and move our legs, but we cannot directly move a tree or push a cloud around the sky. Not only can we move our bodies; the body expresses our personality in its expressions and movements and general properties. We know people's personalities by their bodily gestures and expressions. So the body is not just a tool, to which the spirit is almost externally related; it is also a vehicle for expressing the spirit; it embodies our individual, unique spirit. As Descartes said, in an important but often overlooked phrase, 'The soul is *not* lodged in the body, like a pilot in a ship'; it is interfused with the body completely; the body expresses the spirit, under the conditions of this physical universe.

Secondly, the body, with its organs of sensory perception, acts as a filter or selector of physical stimuli, which cause sense-impressions to arise in the spirit, through action on the brain. Through our bodies, we have direct knowledge of a surrounding part of the world from a certain point of view, within limits set by our sense-organs.

Thirdly, our bodies are subject to physical laws of decay, limitation of power and perception; and much of our awareness must be physically determined by physical states of the brain. It is obvious that we can alter or destroy states of consciousness by affecting the physical structure of the brain. So we say that memories and different aspects of awareness are 'contained in', or depend on, the functioning of various parts of the brain.

Spirit or mind is that which can have knowledge and affective response (feeling) and which can act on the world, think and imagine. The question is: can spirit exist without body? Could there be any being which had direct knowledge of objects (of whatever sort) without possessing any sense-organs? Well, in dreams we have sensory data of the sort that the sense-organs give us, but without the use of such organs. These data probably derived from waking experience, from sense-organs in the first place, but there is no reason why they should not come into our minds directly; sense-organs only provide one possible causal route for providing sense-impressions. So we could have directly caused 'sense-impressions' without any actual senses; that is, without a body.

But how would these impressions be caused? From what point of view would we see them? Who would decide which ones we had? To cut a long story short, let us appeal directly to God. Here is a being who has direct knowledge of everything. He does not even need sense-impressions. He sees from every point of view; he sees the whole universe without any organs of perception; there is nothing unknown to him. Now is such a cosmic mind possible? Obviously, we cannot imagine what such knowledge is like; but I can think of no reason why we should deny its possibility. If God knows everything directly, we could call the whole universe the 'body' of God—as long as we see that it is not a finite part of a larger space, and that it provides no sense-organs; and, of course, it is not essential to God's existence. He could exist without any universe; in which case, he would know his own being perfectly, but there would be nothing else to know. It is probably less misleading to say that the world is not God's body, since the universe does not cause God's mind to deteriorate or grow old, in the way that our bodies do. In any case we can say that there can exist at least one disembodied mind: God, who knows all things directly, and who knows himself perfectly, whether or not anything else exists.

What about action? Could we act without bodies? Again, I do not see why not. Telekinesis—movement of objects by the sheer power of thought, without bodily contact—is certainly conceivable. We could have the power of moving objects in a certain part of space, without actually having observable bodies. There is once more the problem of the causal mechanism involved: what would determine what we could move? Would we not have to have at least position in space? But once more we can appeal directly to God, as a being which has the power to move, or act upon, every part of space directly, without any intervening causal mechanism. It is again probably better to deny that this makes the universe God's body, because there are no physical expressions of God's personality and no analogues of human faces anywhere among the stars. So here is at least one disembodied mind, with the power to act directly on everything.

So it seems that there can be a completely independent disembodied mind, the mind of God. The difficulty with humans is that we are in fact embodied and dependent upon physical laws for our forms of consciousness: and this is necessary, if we are to be members of a causally explicable, emergent world. It seems to be true—and I shall take it as obvious—that awareness is quite a distinct property from any physical properties, and so is different from the physical brain. Moreover, awareness (which I shall call 'spirit') seems to act upon the world through the brain and to be dependent upon the state of the brain for its functioning. There is a two-way causal interaction. Now, can this emergent spirit, being the same individual thing, exist without the body which has generated it? For our last imaginative experiment we will travel through a convenient Black Hole and find ourselves in a world of spirits, where there is no space, and therefore no bodies, at all.

Space is a framework of relations, which are completely transitive and symmetrical and in which each element is related by such relations to each other element; that is, every object in space is related to every other object in space in such a way that each object has a uniquely definable position, with respect to all the others. By using co-ordinates, we can construct a unified map, on which every object has a unique place. It is primarily our position in space, which determines what objects we can know or act upon and what objects we can meet or affect or be affected by. Space provides a way in which objects can be uniquely identified, with respect to one another. People in space can pick each other out and communicate and meet each other by spatial, linear movement.

Now there can be other systems of unified fields of transitive and symmetrical relations, providing for the unique 'location' of objects. Any such system could replace the notion of space, and still contain many identifiable individuals. The easiest such system to think about — it is far from being the only one — is simply a co-ordinated set of numbers. Numbers give a non-spatial method of ordering objects, such that every object has a unique place and is related transitively and symmetrically to every other object within the ordered system (naturally, there can be many different ordered systems of numbers, an infinite number in fact). So we can have an ordered system of numbers, with every individual being assigned a unique number, of which he has direct knowledge.

If I am an individual in such a system, I am potentially related to every other individual in the system. To 'meet' another individual, I have to traverse a sequence of numbers in a certain 'direction' (along a certain axial co-ordinate). Naturally, *my* number remains the same; I am only travelling in thought, or 'counting', so as to contact another individual at a specifically locatable range from me. I will first of all meet spirits at the number-places nearest to mine. But I can no doubt learn to make longer number-journeys in time. I can certainly pick out precisely people at other number-places. But how could we communicate with one another?

The easiest picture is to think of tuning in a radio-receiver. The air is filled with radio-messages, but to receive one of them, I have to tune in to a wave-band (defined by a number or wavelength). When I tune correctly to the number, I receive the message, and only then. If I also have a transmitter, then I can reply to the message by broadcasting on the same wavelength (to the same number-place); and communication is established.

Radio is rather limited; we can only speak. But just the same sort of thing can be done with television, and is quite possible to transmit holographic (fully three-dimensional) pictures to one another. Increase technological capability a little, and we shall be able to transmit sights, sounds, smells and feels, too. There is certainly nothing impossible in the idea. Now, of course, this is all done by physically emanating waves through the atmosphere. In our non-spatial world, such physical waves will be impossible but they will also be unnecessary. Direct telepathy will take their place. The telepathic broadcasting of whole experiences, as well as thoughts and feelings, will be receivable by anyone who tunes to our frequency.

Now there will be no spatial world of which we can have knowledge, but that does not at all mean, as some philosophers have thought, that we shall be confined to earthly memories. We can gain new knowledge in two main ways. First, we can gain it telepathically from one another, receiving their experiences in a much more direct way than we can now. Secondly, there can easily be an 'environment of objects', which are non-spatial in character. In this world, we tune in to number-places simply by thinking them. Many of them are filled by other spirits, which may or may not communicate with us, in various more or less full ways. But we may suppose that many are filled with new sources of experience, perhaps vast and beautiful structures of sound, colour or concept. It is like being in an infinitely large art-gallery-cum-concert-hall-cum-pleasure-dome, or again, it is like having an infinitely channelled television. If we ask what provides these channels, we can no more answer that question than we can say why we see our physical world with colours, sounds, and so on, as we do. There is a physical causal basis for this-worldly perceptions. There will presumably be a non-physical causal basis for our non-space-world perceptions. We can imagine that all possible objects of experience are ranged somewhere along the number-series; so the possibilities are provided simply by the infinite, conceptually ordered mind of God. In the end, for this world and that world alike, we have to say that what we experience is ordered partly by the necessary structure of eternal possibles in God, and partly by his free creative choice.

But the idea of God as the Great Television Producer, and of an after-life as a perpetual television show, seems repulsive. The reason is that, in such a world, we seem to be completely passive, vegetable, unreflective spectators of mere entertainment, without moral value or commitment. However, this is a mistake. Engaged feeling and action are also possible in the non-spatial, non-bodily world. How, without a body? What is needed is the possibility of personal interaction, creative shaping and personal development. The sort of fully enhanced telepathy, of which I have spoken, could accomplish these aims much more fully, in fact, than the very fragile and imperfect actions of our physical bodies. As we communicate with other persons, we could both together visit new environments in their proper number-places. We could creatively transform the sounds, colours and other data (which we obviously cannot imagine, never having had them) into artistic structures. We could engage together in such creative actions building up rich imaginative worlds. We could learn more about others, at a deeper level, and express our own individualities more fully, than ever before. We could enter into a much fuller knowledge, appreciation of others, and learn to co-operate with them in more direct ways, than is ever possible on earth. Maybe our experience could expand until, in some far future, each personal being, at least of a certain sort, could interpenetrate spiritually with others, without losing its individuality. And so unforeseeable possibilities of enrichment would come about, as the infinite universe was explored, without the restrictions imposed by physical decay and spatial distance. This would indeed be a life fit for the gods, where spirit had transcended matter completely, and could yet use it for creative expressions of its own individuality.

But that is enough imagining. I have only wanted to show that non-bodily existence is conceivable and desirable; but it would require very highly developed telepathic control and a great command of conceptually ordered systems. An after-world more commensurate with our rather more mundane and undeveloped spirits would be the resurrection-world postulated by Christian faith. Nevertheless, we can see here some reason for seeing life after death as at least in accord with the nature of things. For such thoughts articulate an intuition as old as human life, that the life of the mind is the true reality of human beings, which the body only partially expresses and partially conceals. In knowledge of oneself, one's own inner being, one seems to find a subjectivity, an inwardness, which is impenetrable by others. This inwardness has resulted from emergent physical evolution, there is no doubt, but it is not explicable physically; it is totally different in kind; it transcends the matter which bore it. Yet so complex has to be the arrangement of matter—in a central nervous system and a brain—to contain consciousness, that we can hardly see it as other than purposively structured towards the birth of spirit. If matter is the womb of spirit and spirit is the purpose of material evolution, with a reality quite different in kind from it; then it becomes reasonable to look for the fulfilment of this purpose in the freeing of spirit from its bonds in a purely spiritual existence.

Mystical religion has borne constant testimony to the experience of such an existence, though the concepts which have been used to describe this experience have varied from culture to culture. It is Christian revelation which defines the form of our freedom, as the fruition of a fully personal and communal life, transfigured by the love of God. But the intuition of such a freedom, in some form, has always haunted the human race. This is not at all a proof of immortality. It may all be no more than imagination, a dream borne from a desperate wish. What I am suggesting is that there is, in consideration of the nature of spirit, its distinction from matter, its intrinsic value and its inner striving towards freedom from and sovereignty over matter, some ground for seeing immortality as a natural possibility of humans. In a materialist view of the universe, immortality must seem odd and implausible, but a view, which places spirit as the centre and purpose of being, can at the very least leave an intelligible place for immortality. It will not seem so odd; one will at least be open to its possibility. When this is taken together with belief in a good and living God, and with that acceptance of Christian revelation, which leads us to affirm the resurrection in a fully physical sense, then immortality becomes a reasonable postulate of faith.

It is still, however, a postulate of faith, and so it must remain. The science-fiction in which I have indulged in this chapter is, for me, a speculative pleasure, but it is not the stuff of religious faith. Its only point has been to show that immortality is not impossible; that, from certain points of view, it may even seem plausible. But I agree with C entirely when he shies away from identifying faith with the acceptance of sheer speculations. There is surely a deep purpose of God in leaving death as a barrier beyond which we cannot go. It need not have been so. It is part of the purpose of this world that we should act and commit ourselves, in ignorance of what, if any, larger context gives overall meaning to our lives. We are asked to commit ourselves to the love of God, in the darkness of suffering and death. We cannot be sure there is no answer to the problem of suffering and that there is no life after death. But our feeble speculations about such things are a poor guarantee of certainty. They may seem plausible to us; yet be dismissed as near-lunacy by our friends (I imagine that would be C's reaction to this chapter). With what, then, are we left? We are left, as C powerfully stresses, with the call to commit ourselves to the way of love and to trust in God, without answers. Where I differ from C is that I take this to be trust in *God*; in a real, objective, existent being, who loves and judges and will save us. And I take it to be *trust* in God; the hope, often despite appearances, that God will bring all to good, that suffering will be done away, and that there will be a full communion of all the saints, in the presence of a God now dimly, then to be clearly, seen. We are called to faith, not, primarily, to philosophy. But that faith is not just some self-commitment without possible issue. It is a relationship of trust and love with the real God who has revealed himself in Jesus Christ. Whether or not we believe in huge talking parrots, Black Holes or amazingly telepathic disembodied minds, it is commitment to and experience of that relationship which will make us say that we look for 'the resurrection of the body, and the life of the world to come'.

# 11

## Salvation

'The main interest of religion,' says C, 'is in the conquest of evil by the transformation of the self' (164). That, I think, is exactly right. But he goes on to say, 'No external object can bring about my inner spiritual liberation . . . only I can free myself'; and it all begins to go wrong. This is one of the things he means by a 'modern and fully autonomous spirituality'; my salvation concerns only the liberation of myself; it can only be brought about by me and it has to be undertaken without any real hope of success. He asks the question himself, 'Is it rational to embrace religion, in view of the seemingly intense unhappiness of many of the most deeply religious and the consequent doubts about how far the religious ideal is attainable?' (116). His answer seems to lie in the stern instruction that we must live the way of purgation just because it is the best way, duty for duty's sake, without extraneous justification. But he is not consistent in giving this answer. He also says 'religion is rational . . . in the sense that the religious consciousness is the mode of consciousness that offers the highest happiness, is capable of the highest virtue, and is the most appropriate to our condition' (161). He does, every now and again, want to appeal to happiness and appropriateness to the facts. But, being fully aware that in this life happiness is hard to come by, and the way of selflessness is hardly appropriate to a world in which we seem to see ruthless competition for the survival of the fittest, he has to fall back on a simple intuitive appeal to the 'sheer rightness' of selflessness. Now I am not even sure that selflessness is the best way to describe the sort of salvation that Christians should be seeking. I am even less sure that we could see such a state to be 'the best', whatever the facts, or the chances of happiness.

C is right in one vital and basic respect: when religion becomes a matter of imposing a set of allegedly correct doctrinal statements on others, it becomes repressive and spiritually sterile. Religion should not be a conservative force, sustaining comfortable prejudices and archaic traditions for their own sake. It should have a disturbing, provocative and critical function, driving us on to new insights and higher ideals. It should be primarily a force for transforming lives and for transmuting earthly life into eternal life. It should put salvation before us, not only as a reward but as a moral challenge.

The Christian Church has one job, which is to preach salvation, but it must be admitted that this has sometimes been seen as implying that the Church should not be involved in political or real life at all. It should simply dispense 'grace' through the sacraments; and when you have accumulated enough grace in your inner bank, then you get salvation in heaven after you die. As far as this world goes, your job, your moral beliefs and so on, the Church keeps out of that (except with regard to sex, strangely enough). Salvation is strictly other-worldly; it comes through ritual, correctly administered; and through the repetition of formulae, correctly remembered.

Now all that is a terrible misrepresentation of what the Church really is, but there is just enough truth in it to be uncomfortable. When we ask what salvation is for the Christian, however, we cannot be content with saying that it is pie in the sky when we die. Nor is it just being saved from hell-fire, which is still rather negative. The biblical images begin with the salvation of the slaves from Egypt, and continue with the salvation of the Israelites from their many enemies and alien rulers in the Holy Land, by Judges and mighty men, raised up by God. It is clear that salvation is a communal thing, not an individual one. It is the whole community which is saved and which is given security in its own land, to develop its own way of life. It certainly involved 'autonomy' in the sense of self-government: that is, being free from oppressors and dictators. Salvation is in history; the Jews did not, for most of the Old Testament period, believe in life after death. The saved community is the community which keeps the Torah, the Law of God. It is a community where justice reigns, and mercy flourishes. So, when the Old Testament speaks of salvation, it speaks of a historical community of justice and mercy, devoted to God, free from oppression; where happiness can be found through the exercise of personal and co-operative gifts and talents.

The three great marks of the saved community are creativity, happiness and love. Creativity, for every person will be able freely to realize his own distinctive personality in creative action.

Happiness, for happiness is not a mere plethora of pleasure; it is well-being, the deep contentment which comes from doing a good job well and from realizing one's proper gifts. So happiness is not some sort of external reward for good conduct. It is the natural affective state of the person who is able to do good, in realizing his proper capacities, the person who successfully brings about the good. Love, because we are not isolated, atomic units, only accidentally related to one another. We only fully become persons when we can appreciate, learn from and work together with others, to form ourselves into a real commonwealth of creative relationships.

Where does God come into this picture? If salvation is a liberation from slavery of all sorts, he certainly cannot come in as yet another dictator or oppressor, however subtle. That is the trouble with C's picture of God. He is a conservative tyrant. He has set up the laws of the world and will not allow them to be changed. He says, 'Hands off my creation; leave it as it is'. He regards any critical or original thought as a manifestation of original sin, of that fall from order which warped the creation. He is our master, and we are his slaves. To serve such a God would be to exchange one form of slavery for another; it would not be salvation at all. But to reject decisively this picture of God is not to reject the true God at all. For that is not the true God; it is a creation of false faith and false religion.

The true God is the being of infinite love, supremely desirable, the ideal who draws the world towards himself by love and who frees us to become co-creators with him in shaping his world. He is the bringer of dreams and the evoker of visions. He has drawn us from the material world, so that we can freely change it. He says, 'Here is my creation; you are an integral part of it; you have the power to shape it; that I freely give to you'. He requires critical and original thought even to understand his revelation truly. He is our lover, and we are his beloved. He does not deprive us of freedom, but he gives our freedom meaning by making our dreams possible.

Philosophers have distinguished two types of freedom, 'freedom from' and 'freedom for'. 'Freedom from' is important, but incomplete. We can be free from oppression and compulsion, but we may still be unable to do many things, because we do not know about them, have not been trained, or have not the money. I am, for example, free from oppression by dictators, but I cannot go to the Bahamas, even though no one is physically stopping me. I just cannot afford it. 'Freedom for' provides the conditions for people to exercise more of their powers, to realize more of their possibilities. It is a positive thing: if I am to go to the Bahamas, you will not only have to stop tying me up; you will actually have to give me the money. Obviously, there can be many degrees of 'freedom for', that is, of positive freedom. We are more free, in this sense, the more things we have the capacity to do, and the more powers and opportunities for their exercise which we have.

Now God does not just leave us free from interference. That is the sort of 'autonomy' that C seems to want. But it is almost laughable to tell a starving, oppressed person that at least he is free from interference by God. What can he actually do? What God does is to enlarge our positive freedom. He provides us with capacities and promises that their fulfilment is possible. In this positive sense, freedom and salvation are the same; when we can fully exercise all our powers in a co-operative community, we shall be free and saved. God gives the powers and makes the community possible. It certainly does not look as if I can do it myself. I might have the power to shape things to some extent and to influence the way they go, but I cannot guarantee that a saved community will ever exist. No finite individual has that much power.

When C says that 'I can only free myself', he has to make salvation an inner, individualistic thing, a matter of my internal consciousness. Yet he recognizes elsewhere that I cannot be saved unless my society is. 'The consciousness of a saint . . . can only become the norm in a classless society of fully-emancipated individuals', he says (146); 'We will not have complete moral integrity until there is such a society'. So he says that there can be no individual salvation without the establishment of the Kingdom of God, the fully just society, which maximizes positive freedom, the fullest compatible exercise of all the powers of rational beings. However, he concludes that we must just do the best we can in the meanwhile; we must aim at our own salvation, as far as possible, and leave it at that. But the whole point is that I cannot just aim at my *own* salvation at all; there is something wrong with the very idea. It is turning salvation into a more subtle form of selfishness.

He says, 'Both Christianity and Buddhism traditionally and correctly insisted that one's first concern must be for one's own salvation' (101). But is that really right? Surely it is Buddhist teaching that the attainment of Nirvana only comes to one who has given up all desire, even desire for salvation? And surely it is Christian teaching that the true—saved—self can only be found by one who gives it up? We might say, following the lines of the argument so far, that our first concern should be with the establishing of a just society, in which alone salvation will be possible for all. But that would not quite go far enough. At least for the Christian, the first concern must be the realization of intrinsic value, of goodness, and that must spring from the reverence for goodness itself, the worship of value, just because it is value. God is both the supremely valuable being and the source of all values; and the first concern of the Christian is to revere God, to delight in his supreme value and to co-operate in realizing in the world those values which only he can make possible and sustain in existence. One's first concern should be God. It is in the perfecting of reverence for God that we will be freed by a vast enlargement of our powers. It is love which frees us to be ourselves.

We can see this in the way in which we feel a vast inflow of creative energy when another person inspires us, encourages us and cares for us. Relationship to other people extends our powers, without in any way impairing our freedom. How much more will a relationship to the supremely valuable being inspire us to realize, by our own creative and imaginative action, the values to which we give particular form in the world around us. We depend upon God for our existence at every moment of our lives. Even though he leaves us free to determine our own future, he has the will and the power to help us if we freely turn to him, not to order us around, but to extend our vision and enhance our powers. Some people think—Communists seem to think—that a perfectly just society can be formed without reference to God. It is, of course, true that we can formulate general principles of justice without explicitly mentioning God, but the well-being of society depends on more than general principles of justice. It depends upon a common vision, upon a deep feeling of fraternity, a belief in the worth-whileness of the communal enterprise, and upon personal relationships of concern and delight, which go far beyond justice.

The Semitic tradition unanimously testifies that the human community can find fulfilment only by conscious obedience to, reverence for and love of God. This is obviously not a conformist obedience to unchangeable, authoritatively revealed laws. It is a transformation of the heart by an object of supreme desirability and value, which cannot be tarnished or shattered by time or circumstance, which can never fail and never will forsake us, which ensures the final, invincible triumph of love. In Christianity, the written laws of the Torah point the way beyond themselves, to an annulment which is also their transformation, to the person of Christ. It is that person who inspires us to new visions and who mediates to us the personal reality of God. To separate ourselves off from that personal reality, which is the very source of our existence, which shows itself to us in guiding love and to try to live out of our own strength, without reliance on that freely offered love, is to choose the way to the far country of desolation and eventual death. For once we have rejected the root and source of love, we have nothing left to give to others. We become slaves of our own fear and rage. We become unable to love, because we have turned away from the springs of love. The reason why a just society cannot exist without God is that we all rely, for our deepest motives and resources, on inner, hidden springs, far below conscious reasoning. We all express our own inward relation to the reality which bore us. And if we are uprooted from love, we simply will not have the resources to relate to others in the open and unresentful ways that justice requires. A just society can only be founded by good men. A man is good only if he is both strong and loving, without any hint of fear or resentment, without needing to dominate others or to surrender his personality to others, to be a master or a slave. Such strength and love can, in the end, only come from the One who has infinite strength and love, the creator of all things.

Does this mean that we need God only as a crutch or prop for our weakness? That very way of putting the question reveals the deepest human fear—the fear of appearing 'weak', dependent, cringing, servile. It is as if we ought to be able to do it on our own, but unfortunately, we need to ask God for help—how humiliating. It is this talk of 'going it alone', which is so absurd and so self-deceiving. Suppose you ask a person who is married to someone he loves dearly, whether he needs his spouse only as a prop for his weakness. Surely he would say that he *could* live alone. But it is hardly weakness to find love in companionship with another. He might say that it is only when the couple acknowledge their due dependence on one another—but also their proper independence as separate persons—that they can fulfil themselves. But speaking of it as a 'prop for weakness' misses the whole point. It is really an acknowledgement of the fact that fulfilment comes through due dependence. So it is with God. We are in fact dependent on God at all times. It would be absurd to deny it, and when we see that there is a proper independence too, since we are distinct persons, we should be crazy not to find our fulfilment in that dependence. Can we be wholly dependent while not being servile, while we retain a proper uniquely personal creative freedom? If God is omnipotent love, then that would be the only appropriate way to be. Only the establishing of such a relationship would constitute true self-knowledge. Only then could we have a fully honest perception of ourselves. Only if we are fully honest and self-accepting, can we form part of the truly just society. God is necessary for a just society, just because the whole universe, which gives rise to the possibility of such a society, and which defines our basic natures as both dependent and responsible, is an expression of omnipotent love. To fail to recognize that fundamental fact would be to miss the truth about our own deepest natures, and that would make the establishing of a just order in society impossible.

It is no accident that in a world which is alienated from God by sin, justice seems in fact to be impossible. The more we aim at it, the more we are corrupted by passion and injustice and violence. In a world like this, talking about the Kingdom of God coming on earth seems hopelessly idealistic. If salvation is to be communal and in history, then it is impossible. It is only if I think of myself as somehow being able to extract myself from history and live through millions of lonely lifetimes, that I can think of saving myself. It has been a feature of the Indian tradition, and of some periods of Christianity, like the age of the Desert Fathers, that the world must be left to go to the Devil, while I can sit on top of a pole and pull myself painfully into a private state of 'salvation'. That is a complete perversion of the Christian idea, which continues the Jewish insight that purely personal salvation is impossible. The trouble is that social salvation seems to be impossible, too.

Christianity has sought various ways of coping with this difficulty, but central to all of them is the firm belief that it is Jesus Christ who is the only saviour of humanity, the only one who can bring about a saved, fulfilled, just society at all. How he does this has been subject to varied interpretations, but that he, and he alone, does it, has never been in doubt. It has been generally agreed among Christians that salvation will never come about on earth by human effort. The human race, bound together by indissoluble bonds, suffers the consequences of generations who have turned from God, from love and thus from justice. Children grow up today in a society, whose very structures reflect selfish desire and corrupt reason. They can hardly expect to escape its influence. So, not knowing God clearly or being able to do even what they know to be right, they helplessly follow the path of alienation from God. That is 'original sin': the helplessness of humans in a world that has turned from God. However much we would like to turn to God and to follow him truly, we cannot do so. The greatest of the saints testify that they too feel a yawning gulf between what they should be and what they are. Salvation remains, humanly speaking, impossible.

It is not enough, Christians would say, to follow the Buddhist way. That is the private way of the renunciation of all desire: leaving the world, renouncing temptation, seeking complete disinterest in all things. For a Christian, this will never accomplish salvation. It is a turning from God's purpose, his positive purpose of shaping a good world. It is, as indeed Buddhists sometimes say, a sort of death, a sort of suicide, a renouncing of life. But God has given life; it is a gift; and to renounce it is to spurn his gift. It is to evade responsibility; to escape a sense, a knowledge of failure, by no longer attempting anything. Christians have almost always rejected this way, except for the very few; and it has refused to call those few a spiritual élite. They are, in a sense, the weak; for the better way is to try to show love in the world, and to live with failure, in pursuit of the good.

So we know what salvation is; we know we cannot achieve it; we know we must live with failure, however well-intentioned we are. That is the beginning of Christian faith. For it means that we realize that we need forgiveness, reconciliation and redemption. We know, indeed, that only God can give us these things; and yet how can God give them without impugning that freedom which he has first given? If we go on failing, and causing great evil and suffering, as we do, by our thoughtlessness and greed, how can God just say, 'Don't worry; it will be all right'? What can he really do, that will enable us to live with our failure, without somehow condoning it or lessening its terrible force? How can he reconcile us to himself, when we daily turn from him? How can he redeem us from the power of evil, when we freely put ourselves within that power, time and again? We might realize that we need to be saved; but how can we be, if our freedom is exercised in the service of evil?

It is quite wrong to think that I can save myself; I am helpless to do so. Only God can save, but how can he do so, if, in his love, he preserves our freedom, even to reject him? Now the Christian faith has no neat, simple answer to this question. It does not really tell us *how* God can. It tells us *that* God did, in the life of Jesus and especially by the cross. On the cross, Jesus offered his life, as a sacrifice for our sins, to ransom us from the power of evil. Now clearly, if this was just the offering of a human life, it could not accomplish such a purpose. There have been many noble self-sacrifices; but they could hardly redeem the whole world from sin. Such talk is ludicrous, unless what was offered was much more than a human life; and the clue to the Christian doctrine of salvation is that what was offered was not the death of a man, but the life of God. It was not, as it has been caricatured, that God sent his Son to be tortured and killed, to satisfy his own injured dignity. That way of speaking assumes that God's Son is somebody else. Whereas the Son of God is God himself, an indivisible part of the Holy Trinity. It is God's own life which is offered in the death of Jesus.

Through the crucifixion, God himself was somehow able to share in the experience of human suffering and death. 'He has borne our griefs and carried our sorrows' (Isa. 53.4); he knows from the inside what it is to be human and suffering. 'He was wounded for our transgressions'; it was human sin which brought this experience upon God. 'Upon him was the chastisement that made us whole, and with his stripes we are healed'; somehow this free act of God, in suffering with us and because of us, makes us whole and accomplishes our salvation.

How can the self-offering of God, his sharing in our suffering, make us whole? To be saved, to be made whole, the human heart needs to be changed radically from within. It is enmeshed in a world of greed, pride and fear, incapable even of true, lasting repentance and trust. We do not just exist alone, as individuals, unaffected by those around us. Our relationship to society is closer than that, and we stand in solidarity with a community enslaved by sin and by alienation from God, from one another and from our deepest selves. Evil must be conquered; but not as some external force. It must be conquered in ourselves, by the transformation of self. Everything in us that erects a barrier between us and God must be removed; that is what it means to say that 'our sins must be taken away'.

Now evil cannot be taken from us by some external act; that would be an invasion of our freedom. No doubt God could make us all morally perfect overnight, using his omnipotence just to change our characters completely, but that would contradict his love, which wills to leave us free and morally mature individuals. What, then, can God do to change our deepest motivations, without restricting our freedom?

The first thing that he can do is to overcome the alienation, the separation which we have brought about between ourselves and him. He can overcome it by freely entering into our situation, in weakness and not in power, taking upon himself the worst that our sinful natures can do. By offering himself as man, freely accepting in his own person the consequences of our evil, God overcomes the gulf that we have opened. In fear and resentment of an omnipotent God, we create a world in which we try to live alone, out of our own strength, but all we do is create a world of ignorance and disordered desire, of suffering and death, seen as a threat and as a denial of all our hopes and plans. It is in this very world that we find God again, but not as an omnipotent power, blasting aside the frail structures of selfishness that we have erected, in wrath and judgement. We find him as a love which will never leave us, however far we travel, trying to take leave of it. This love has, indeed, a power that we can never take from it; we cannot conquer or exterminate it; it lives on, despite the worst that we do to it. But it never uses this power to compel; it uses its power to endure and to go on loving, even when taking upon itself the greatest suffering that we can inflict. We see God truly when we see that enduring, accepting love which never compromises nor accepts defeat but is never resentful or unforgiving. This is the first healing, a healing of vision. The tyrant God of our disordered sight is revealed as an ogre of our own imagining. The true God is seen on the cross, a love as strong as death, invincible in endurance.

That vision brings us to repentance, as it makes clear to us what we are doing to ourselves, and what we are doing to God. It makes clear the lengths to which divine love will go, to bring us back to itself. So it can begin to transform us. The conquest of evil begins in the vision of love. It is that which begins to break down the walls of self we have so elaborately built around ourselves. It is not the desire of heaven or the fear of hell, which leads us to turn to God; in them the tortuous voice of prudence still inserts itself. What leads us to turn to God is the true vision of his patient, endless love, as the crucified Lord of Glory with arms outstretched in pain and blessing over the world. 'He bore our sins in his own body on the tree'; and all the attraction of sin for us fades before this apprehension of its consequence.

The cross shows the lengths to which God goes to gain our repentance, which breaks the grip of evil over us; but we still need to be made one with him, and that we are still too weak to do. Indeed, it is obvious that, if there is a God, only he could establish a full personal relationship, a one-ness with his creatures. This he does in an amazingly new way, by the presence of the living Christ and through the Holy Spirit, in the life of the individual believer. Our trust in God is our acceptance of a living union with Christ. It is not just the intellectual belief that Jesus rose from the death and lives in some strange sense. It is a living relationship with the risen Christ. I believe this to be the true foundation of Christianity, its real heart. God can transform you through the presence of Christ within.

When C speaks of the 'three converging themes', which lead us to cease to speak of God in cosmic or objective terms, his third theme is what he calls the 'New Covenant'. He says that the divine requirement cannot remain 'an objective authority external to man which tries to control him from without' (4). It needs a 'complete inner transformation of human nature which cannot be brought about from outside'. 'God must put his spirit into our hearts'. Well, that is absolutely right; but how could it possibly lead us to stop speaking of God in objective terms? How could it possibly be compatible with saying that man is completely autonomous? C says, 'The power that brings about my inner transformation must be fully internalized until it springs up at the very source of my own affections and will' (5). But there *is* a power. That power cannot control us 'from without', without our consent, as a power clearly distinguishable from ourselves. The power must work at the source of our affections and will; it must so co-operate with ourselves that we cannot clearly distinguish where our activity begins or ends. But there is a co-operation with this power of God within our minds and hearts.

Christians say, 'Not I live, but Christ lives in me', and 'The self is hidden with Christ in God'. They do not mean that Christ is not a real objective power. They do mean that the power of Christ is known at the heart of the self, transforming it in such a way that our individual wills co-operate so closely with his that we cannot clearly tell them apart. There is not a complete merger, and the process is very fitful, for all of us. It is that power to transform us, to make us grow in love, which *is* the spiritual life, for Christians. Salvation becomes union with Christ; that is, it is union with the power of God to help us grow in love, which was fully expressed in Jesus. It comes to us in the 'form' of Jesus; as we meditate upon the records of his life and teachings and seek to think of God by thinking of him, so God's Spirit comes to us, impressed with the personality of Jesus. These things are almost impossible to describe, but I am certain that there is a power of God to make us whole by growth in deep personal relation with him. This is the power of love, and it comes to us fully and properly in the form of Jesus, the risen Christ.

If you speak like this, you are committed to speaking of God in cosmic or objective terms. Once again, C is rejecting the external God, who commands and expects us to obey, in favour of a God who loves, and asks us to respond, and who can make his presence felt in the stillness of our innermost selves. But he is not really rejecting God at all; is simply insisting on the greater adequacy of a truly Christian idea of God. That idea is of a God who becomes man, who suffers and dies; who expresses his being for ever in the form of the risen and glorified Christ; and who transforms our personalities from within, by our free and co-operative consent, into the image and likeness of that Christ. This is the second healing, a healing of the will. Our weakness and helpless bondage to evil is transformed by the power of God, by a real and personal and growing union with Christ.

By repentance and faith—this living trust in the power of God—we are on the way to salvation, but it remains obviously true that in this world we are never saved. The saved community never comes into being, and churches which have been sometimes tempted to identify themselves with 'the saved' have always come in for a nasty shock. We can dare to speak of evil being conquered and the self being transformed, but we must be clear that it is always partial, never complete. We still long for the accomplishment of salvation and we still need repentance, to the last moment of our lives. When will salvation come?

Christians are generally agreed that it will come in the fellowship of all the saints before the vision of God, that is, in a world beyond this, when the truly just community can come to fruition. In this sense, salvation is heaven. It is not, however, a reward for work well done. It is the fulfilment of God's promises, that his will for creation is to be accomplished, despite human evil, and its immense cost. Again, only God can make such salvation possible; nothing less than omnipotence could ensure it. But again, divine omnipotence leaves humans free. Having loved to the uttermost and offered his transforming power, God can do no more than promise to those who turn to him, that they will see the Kingdom of God in reality. But he leaves people free not to turn; and if they do not, they must continue to live in the world they have preferred to make for themselves. This world is described in the New Testament as a rubbish-heap, an outer darkness, an exclusion from a joyful feast. It is hell, a hell that people make for themselves, if they reject all that God does and offers. C rejects contemptuously a God who says, 'Love me; and if you do not, I will roast you in hell for ever'. But the God revealed in Christ says, 'See, I do all that I can to turn your hearts to love. There is no more even I can do, if you are to be free. You are leading yourselves to destruction. With all the power love can command, I implore you to turn back, before it is too late'. Here is no threat by an arbitrary autocrat. Here is a cry from the cross, to try to save men from self-destruction.

When Christians say that only Jesus Christ can save mankind, they mean that only the love of God, which is fully and definitively expressed in Jesus Christ—and which will be expressed in him for all eternity—can bring men into the kingdom of justice and perfect truth. There will be such a community, though not in this world. All those who turn to God will belong to it. If this is not true, then talk of salvation is a sham, and the Christian gospel is a delusion. C's attempt to speak of salvation as a purely individual, unachievable state in this life is not a 'more mature' spiritual view. It is just an attempt to keep on using the word, when everything important about the concept has been given up.

Does such an idea of salvation as other-worldly mean that we will see this world as unimportant and not really worth bothering with? Not at all. For turning to God is something with real, hard practical consequences for here and now. It requires the most earnest efforts after truth and justice; for 'any man who says he loves God, but does not love men, is a liar' (1 John 4.20). This world takes on a greater importance, when we see that people's choices here are relevant, not just for a few years, but for an eternal life. What we do here and now becomes of literally eternal consequence. That is hardly regarding this world as unimportant. However, there is a point here; it is that we should not be too depressed or anxious about what our efforts will actually accomplish. We must strive as hard as we can, but the consequences of our acts are not limited to this world; so what seems to be success or failure here is of little account in eternity. Jesus even teaches that those who weep will be comforted, and those who are rich now, will be poor. The point is not a literal one, but it is real, nonetheless. That is, good acts will have consequences, even if they apparently fail in this world; the cross is a good example of that. Though evil may seem to conquer here, its defeat is certain, for Christ has accomplished salvation from its power. Thus we must act, but leave the consequences of our actions in God's hands. That is part of the meaning of faith; that having done all we can, we must leave the outcome, that we cannot help, to God in trust that good will triumph.

This is the third healing, a healing of the world's sorrow, the triumph of good. Though our world is bent on self-destruction, God will save and make whole and establish securely a community within which love and justice can grow and flourish. That is salvation, in the Christian view. Salvation may be lost. But if so, it will be by a free personal choice against love and the self-transcendence that love requires. If it is, by anyone, utterly and finally lost, I believe that the ultimate end of that person will be his ceasing to be a person at all: the complete, self-willed disintegration of his personal being into utter nothingness. I also believe, however, that Christ came to redeem the whole world from sin. Therefore we may rightly pray that all may be saved, but not even the omnipotence of God can guarantee that, if human freedom remains the condition of love. What we should pray is that all the good there is in creation should be conserved; that it may extend and flourish; and that all the creatures of God may rejoice in it. We pray for the coming of God's Kingdom, which is the salvation of the world. We believe that it will come; for God was in Christ, reconciling the world to himself. That incarnating of love in a fallen world goes far beyond the calm, dispassionate ordering of the world by a Creative Ideal, of which I have already spoken. It adds a new dimension to our thought of God, to see him as enfleshed in suffering, expressed for ever in human form. The Christian God is the incarnate God; because he enters into our infirmity, we are made whole in him. The main interest of religion is in the conquest of evil by the transformation of the self. Only the incarnate, suffering God, the God who reigns in glory from the cross, has the weakness and the power to do that.

# 12

## Christ and Other Religions

It should be apparent by now that C has invented a new religion. There is nothing wrong with that. It is something most of us are tempted to do, at one time or another, when we get fed up with our friends and colleagues. Very few people agree exactly with others on every point, however orthodox they all claim to be, and whether you think your differences amount to a new religion or not is partly a matter of taste. Is Methodism the same religion as Roman Catholicism? The same religion as Quakerism? Is humanism a religion? Or Marxism? There are no absolutely hard and fast lines; and it is Western Europeans, with their liking for pigeon-holes, who have defined the 'world-religions' for us.

Still, though that is true, some forms of religion seem to be very different from others, and if most people were asked which two generally acknowledged religions were furthest apart from each other, I think they would say Buddhism and Christianity. Buddhism has no God, no prayer, no personal immortality, no salvation, no interest in Jesus. Christianity says that people can be given eternal life, but only by Jesus. That seems about as far apart as you can get. Yet C seems to recommend something that he calls 'Christian Buddhism'. The Christian Buddhist, he says, 'has one very strong point in his favour: he is much closer to people of other faiths than is his doctrine-affirming critic. His religion may not be fully universal but at least it is a great deal less parochial than the other's' (83). I am not sure about this last point. Since I suspect that there are only a very few Christian Buddhists in the world (maybe only one), it seems a very parochial religion indeed, and, while he claims to be closer to Buddhists than more traditional Christians, I suspect that he would get very short shrift from most Buddhists.

What is Christian Buddhism? He hints at something 'Buddhist in form, Christian in content' (xiii), but he may as well have put these words the other way around, since there turns out to be not much Christian content left. He speaks of someone, who is at least agnostic about the doctrinal aspects of Christianity, but who wants to cultivate 'the ethics, the inwardness, the spirituality and many of the ritual practices' of Christianity. He wants to study the words of 'that great spiritual master, Jesus'. He would have no doctrine, but be very saintly.

Despite the fact that I think this approach wholly misconceived, I do see the attraction of it. I hope that I am far from being a blind dogmatist myself; and I have moved towards a fairly traditional Christian view from a position of complete atheism, while I was teaching philosophy in British universities. It is the speculative doctrines of Christianity, especially when formulated in terms of outdated (or at least very ancient) philosophical systems, which are difficult. To become Christians, we seem to have to take on board a very complicated philosophy and become involved in disputes about angels on the heads of pins, substances changing while accidents remain the same and three natures, persons and substances, which are all the same and yet different at the same time. It is all very confusing and not very relevant. When we look at people arguing about such things, we may well wonder if it is making them more saintly or not rather more bad-tempered and disputatious.

So I absolutely agree that Christianity is not primarily a bit of ancient philosophy, or even a bit of Victorian sexual repression (which it can also resemble). It is really about a person, a person who, over all these years, and for all the tiny amount written about him, upon which all our knowledge of him depends, compels our attention, provokes and fascinates us and cannot be made simply to go away. It is about Jesus, who taught that God, the creator of all things, was a forgiving, loving, personal God, who was bringing his rule near in the person of Jesus himself. Jesus called men to follow him; he healed the sick and taught with authority; he asked for absolute allegiance; and, most important of all, he appeared to his disciples after he had been cruelly killed. Inflamed with a new power and joy, these disciples began to preach throughout the known world that God had come near to them in Jesus, and that he was with them still, in a new way, through his Spirit.

These facts are well known. But we need to recall that our faith is in the person of Jesus as the revelation of almighty God, and in the new life which he himself brings. It is not a philosophy, not a doctrine, not a 'spirituality', whatever that is. It is *the very life of God brought near in the person of Jesus*: vibrant, alive, compelling. In one way, therefore, it is the most simple faith, available to the simplest person. There is not much doctrine in it at all. But of course there is an enormous amount of doctrine underlying it. Once we begin to ask, Is there a personal God? What do we know about Jesus? How can we know it is Jesus we seem to experience now? Is life after death possible? Then we get into doctrine, in a big way. Somebody has to deal with those problems.

Now is Buddhism really very different in this respect? It is possible to be a very simple Buddhist—just to meditate, accept the teachings in the Scriptures, seek detachment from all desires; but underlying these practices there is an enormous amount of subtle and difficult philosophy, about the nature of the self, the nature of ultimate reality, the causes of suffering, reincarnation and so on. It is true that Gautama Buddha did not encourage his disciples to ask questions about the gods, but the reason for that is that he did not regard the gods as very important; they were no more than superhuman spirits, a long way from ultimate reality. All the same, Buddhism is not just a system of meditation, without any doctrine. There is a complex and difficult doctrine of no-self, karma, suffering, Nirvana, and a commitment to the truth of certain historical claims: for example, that the Lord Gautama, or at least somebody, achieved Enlightenment, and so taught the way to it truly and authoritatively.

C's picture of Buddhism as a non-doctrinal way of spirituality is far from the truth and vastly over-simplified. The 'Pure Land' school and to a lesser extent, most Mahayana schools of Buddhism (which are very strong, relatively speaking) regard the Buddha as a personal saviour and hope for personal immortality. In such schools, the average believer probably reveres the gods, regards the Buddha as his saviour, and tries to build up merit for future lives. The very agnostic schools, which regard meditation simply as a technique for achieving inner calm and enhanced perception here and now, are hardly religious at all. They are more like subtle forms of self-hypnosis. There is no need to object to them as techniques, but a Christian will have every reason for insisting that the 'calming of the mind' is not the ultimate object of human life; indeed, it leaves life without a point. It has little to do with 'salvation', even in the main Buddhist traditions, where Nirvana is spoken of as absolute bliss and freedom. It has no conception of a personal God or of redemption by a self-offering of divine love.

Of course, we should want to be calm, loving, dispassionate and patient under stress. We should also want to be active in love, passionate for justice and concerned for the poor and helpless. We should want to see reality truly, so that we may react to it appropriately, whether by rejection of its ruthless amorality (if that is the truth) or by acceptance of its self-giving love (if that is nearer the mark). The different world-religions present to us rather different pictures of reality, and so of the appropriate response to it. In each, there is a spiritual ideal, an ideal of the holy, fully human, life. It is helpful to stress that each of these ideals seeks to state what human moral perfection is; and it is a terrible perversion when their pursuit seems to lead to moral imperfection, such as intolerance of others. But it is necessary also to stress that the ideals are different, and cannot be simply merged, however ecumenical that may seem to be.

The Christian ideal has perhaps been unduly narrowed and over-simplified in Western European thought. It should present the ideal as a maturing of humanity through a sharing in the creative life of God. Through the sacraments of the Church, we should find growing unity with the infinite divine reality, and through the icon of the person of Jesus Christ, we should find a way to a truly appropriate relation with the mystery of the self-existent One. A sense of the mystery and infinity of God should be balanced by a recognition of his self-revelation in the person of Jesus, and now, through the sacramental mystery of the Church, the body of Christ. This self-revelation should lead us to participate as co-creators in shaping the world freely and imaginatively, as we grow together in a community of the Spirit.

Unfortunately, the picture can be drawn in a different way. Faith can be fearful and restrictive; it can suppress what seems to threaten it and caution us against interfering with the ways of God. So it can become a repressive and conservative force. It can present Jesus as an all-too-accessible human being, and thus induce a naive view of prayer as chatting to an invisible friend, and a view of God as a being very much made in our parochial image. Seeing that faith is open to the simple, it can make a virtue out of naivety, and make the most absurd statements about things about which it knows nothing, such as biology and astronomy. Or it can fail altogether to see that there is such a thing as growth in spiritual insight and maturity, and insist on taking the newest, simplest believer as the paradigm of the Christian. The possible mistakes are many, as in every field of human endeavour, and with every form of religion: and one valuable way of correcting one's most natural mistakes is to look to other forms of sincere and intellectually subtle and spiritually fruitful religion. There we may find prompts to lead us to see treasures in our own tradition we have missed.

If God is everywhere guiding people to an insight into his own reality, no great religion will be without the touch of God's grace. None will be just wrong, in its entirety. Each will have something of great, and maybe unique, value to contribute to our understanding of God. It would be a terribly restrictive view of God's love to say that he had only revealed himself in one tradition and not at all to others. We must believe, then, that something of God is truly seen in all the great religious traditions.

But it is senseless to say that all are equally true. The old story of the men feeling different parts of an elephant, which is usually trotted out at this point, rarely leads people to draw the obvious conclusion, which is that it really *is* an elephant, after all. One person feels the trunk, another the legs, another the tail; all guess it to be different animals, but it really is an elephant, all the same. Now there is no reason to assume that God is so unknowable that we could never know what he is truly like. It would need a very sophisticated argument to show that was true, and Christians have traditionally taught that we do see what God is truly like, in Jesus. Obviously, we do not know everything about him, and we do not have a 'God's-eye view' of him, whatever that would be. But we do know something finally and completely true about him, as he appears in human form.

It does at first sight sound more tolerant to say that all the great religions are wrong about God, or have partial insights. All cannot be true, we might say, but all can be equally false, or partial. We would all have to say, 'God is not in fact what I think; but that is how he seems to me'. Now this will do for some sorts of talk about God, but not for most of it. For instance, one person may say that God is more like a man; others that 'he' is more like a woman. Both may agree that God himself has no sex ('himself' is too difficult to drop, here), but insist that their strictly incorrect view still says something about how God appears to them, respectively. This would be rather like preferring different sorts of paintings or music. It expresses an attitude often found among

Indians to their gods—if you do not like one, try another. To the extent that it is a matter of preference for symbolism or evocative poetry, we can see different religions as different 'pictures' of God, each with its own local appeal.

Symbolism is very important in religion. I think we come to a knowledge of the divine reality through taking things or events as symbols of transcendent reality; and non-literal symbolism always remains of great importance. The trouble is, however, that not all our religious beliefs are purely matters of symbolism. Truth-claims about the nature of the physical universe and about the destiny of human beings are also involved, as well as more difficult claims about the nature of ultimate reality, which are not merely symbolic. For example, even sticking at the vaguest possible level, a philosophy of materialism would not allow for the existence of a transcendent divine reality at all, so it would contradict almost all religious views. We could not seriously claim that it merely presented a different symbolic picture of the world. Either there is a God to be symbolized or there is not.

C confuses this issue by going on using talk about God: 'God is a myth we have to have', he says (166); while at the same time saying that 'there is no objective personal God' (93). God, for him, becomes a non-existent ideal, which sets before us the ultimate end of a perfected human life, as far as I can tell. So it makes no ontological claim at all: no claim to refer to an objective existent reality. Well, if that is true, then all the different doctrines about God in the different religions are not contradicting each other—that is, they are not saying different things about the same thing at the same time—because they are not saying anything about anything. We can all have different religious ideals. We shall certainly disagree in our ways of life, but we cannot be contradicting each other, because none of us are any more claiming to tell the truth, or to have any truth to tell.

The trouble is that all that C is really doing here is contradicting most known religious opinions. He may very well invent for himself, autonomously, an ideal way of life, and get on with it. He may, if he wishes, tell himself false stories about non-existent gods to help him follow his ideal (though that sort of help seems rather dubious). What he cannot do is tell people like me what I *really* mean when I speak of God. Words mean what fully educated, competent language-speakers intend them to mean. I intend the word 'God' to refer to the perfect creator of the universe, and the dictionary assures me, if in doubt, that it does mean just that. There might be no such being, but I think there is, and I mean to refer to it. I simply do not use the word 'expressively' rather than 'descriptively' or 'referringly'. While I may be making a factual mistake about God's existence, I am certainly not making a logical mistake, by any known rules of logic or semantics. So, if C insists on using the word 'God' expressively and non-referringly, he is involved in a factual dispute with me and all my fellow-believers. We say there is a God, and he says there is not (or that we could not refer to one, if there was). It is not just that we are using words in different ways (though we are). We are disagreeing about the facts, about the nature of the world.

We must insist, then, that it is possible to contradict religious doctrines. They are not all purely symbolic or expressive or non-truth-claiming. The opinion that they are, is itself a truth-claim which contradicts the beliefs of most, nearly all, theists. So it is self-refuting. To the extent that a religion embodies truth-claims, these claims can be contradicted. Where two views are contradictory, only one of them can be true, though both can be false, logically. Now such claims may be difficult to decide; and we may not feel called upon to decide all of them. But sometimes we have to choose, and then we are forced to say that we accept one doctrine as true, and reject the other as false. It is subterfuge, which helps no one, to say that both of them are partially true.

To come to the important point, traditional Christian doctrines are that the world is freely created by a personal God, who loves his creation; that Jesus of Nazareth was the full expression of God's love in the world, and the one through whom the world is re-united to the love of God; and that the purpose of human life is that persons should be united in an everlasting fellowship with God, through the risen and glorified Christ. There is a lot of symbolism involved in Christianity, and a lot of non-literal talk about Jesus 'sitting at God's right hand', 'coming on clouds of glory' and so on, but there is also a lot of factual content. There are claims about the nature of ultimate reality, about human history and about human destiny. If these are given up, then naturally we will be closer to other religions which do not have them. But what if they happen to be true?

At first it looks as if there are two main options open to us. We can say that every religion so far has been false, and we must start a new one. This is, in effect, what C does; and it does not matter much whether he calls it 'Christian Buddhism', 'Hindu Islam' or 'Atheistic theism'; it will be a new, and allegedly better, religion, which will disagree with all the others. Or we can say that one of the religions is true, where the others contradict it, and all the others are false. This may look less tolerant, at first sight; but it is not, in fact; it is actually more tolerant, because it disagrees with one less religion than the first option.

However, putting the options like this is much too simple. Religions are not things that can be considered wholesale. Each one has hundreds of sub-sects and hundreds of more-or-less important doctrines. It is rather senseless to ask if the whole of Christianity is true, when Roman Catholics cannot even agree with Anglicans. We have to take doctrines one by one. As we work through them, we may well find particular doctrines from other religions, which shed new light on our own views and help to broaden and deepen them. Tolerance may be practised by listening attentively to what others say and respecting sincere differences of belief. We neither have to pretend to accept everybody's views (which is impossible) nor reject everybody's, in the sense in which they believe them.

The view which I believe to be true and which therefore is bound to colour my whole attitude to this matter, is as follows: God has revealed himself truly in Jesus and has redeemed us through Jesus. The self-giving love shown on the cross truly shows what God is like. We are destined for eternal life, if we repent and have faith (respond to the inward power of the Spirit of Christ in us). Now I also think that it follows from this view of God as supreme love that he will not have left any people wholly without knowledge of him. How can we believe both of these things?

First, we can say that God reveals something of himself everywhere, in the beauty and order of nature, in providence and answered prayer, in moral challenge and inner spiritual strength. God is never absent from his creation. But he does not reveal himself in the same way or to the same extent everywhere. It is in Jesus (who was himself the culmination of a long process of preparation in the history of Israel) that God gives the full disclosure of himself. At that point of history, the conditions were uniquely right for such a disclosure, in a way they never were or would be elsewhere. Just as the Old Testament prepares the way for that revelation, so we can see the other great religious traditions as preparing the way for a deeper understanding of it. In the Indian traditions, the emphasis came to be on the unity of all being, on the path of meditation and dispassionateness, on the inner union of the self and the ultimate reality 'beyond name or form'. There are in these traditions great correctives to certain Christian limitations. Christians have sometimes viewed animals and nature as just objects to be used, things without souls, not worthy of respect. A stress on the unity of all being, as an expression of God, will correct this mistake of exaggerating the importance of the human species. Sometimes, too, Christian prayer has remained at a naive level of asking God for things, without enough stress on contemplation and self-discipline. It should not have done so, but again, the Indian emphasis on holiness and wordless prayer can remind us that there is more to prayer than talking, and it is possible that Christians have sometimes stressed the transcendence, the otherness of God, so much that he becomes an external, remote power. The Indian traditions preserve a clear sense of the intimate presence of God to the self, of the divine immanence.

So there are real insights into the nature of God in the Indian traditions, which Christians can learn from with great profit. They have their way to God; and we can learn from it. Nevertheless, we cannot compromise on the belief that God has acted in Christ. This belief involves three elements which the Indian traditions understress or ignore: first, the importance of community, of social justice and active love in relation to one another; secondly, the importance of history and of a positive and good purpose in creation, within which humans have a creative and responsible role to play; thirdly, the importance of morality, of individual responsibility and commitment to truth and justice. All these elements flow from the belief that God has acted in history, calling us to renewed moral sensitivity and commitment, to work for the Kingdom of God.

We can indeed seek for a form of religious life, which can include the complementary insights from Indian and Semitic traditions. What we cannot do is to renounce our belief in God's objective revelation of himself in Christ. If we did that, our spiritual lives would no longer be a response to God. They would be a form of psychological self-help. I am all for people getting any help they can, from wherever they can. But if God has made us to find fulfilment in response to him, by sharing in his love, we shall not get any lasting help that does not come from God himself. We cannot afford to turn away from that.

A more difficult problem for Christians than the existence of a very ancient Indian tradition of religion, is the existence of Judaism and Islam. They have both seen Christianity at close quarters, and turned away. What are we to make of that? Well, we cannot just say that they have seen the truth and rejected it, as though that truth was clear and compelling. The Christian claims can, as I have said, be accepted by simple people; but they are in themselves very complex and capable of many interpretations. They probably do not appear as real options to most Jews and Muslims and never have done. We know that any philosophical, moral, religious or political doctrine will attract some people and not others. We know that the reasons for attraction will be many and varied (from a liking for the vicar to an acceptance of a Neo-platonic world-view). The presentation of Christian claims by us does not have the character of a luminously clear and irrefutable argument. It is mixed up with our own biases and partialities; it reflects our own temperament and culture. Similarly, it is heard by people of a certain temperament and culture, with certain predispositions and beliefs, which must be modified or changed if they are to accept what we say. I am not intending to leave out of account the Spirit of God here. But the Spirit does not move as we would like or predict; and he may often work in ways which would surprise or shock us. To take a small example, the division of the Kingdom of Israel into two ineffectual petty states looked clean contrary to God's purposes; yet he himself willed it, so we are told (cf. 1 Kings 12). We cannot see the interplay of human freedom, social interaction and divine grace which guides events, with any clarity. We certainly do not believe that everything that happens is what God wants. But we do believe that he can use whatever happens for good in the long run (yes, maybe when we are dead).

So we do not know why so many Jews rejected Jesus as Messiah. But it would be totally misleading, even dangerously so, to call it a conscious rejection of God's revelation. It was probably sincerely seen by most as just the rejection of yet another messianic heresy. The Jews remain the chosen people, still set apart by God for his purpose. The writer of the letter to the Romans wrestles with this problem and concludes that the rejection of Jesus by the

Jews has the purpose of releasing Christianity to be a world-religion, a faith for the Gentiles, but in the end, he supposes, all the Jewish people will find their true role again; their special destiny is not revoked (Rom. 11.25-6). Christians see the history of Israel as a preparation for the revelation of the love of God in Christ. But that love comes in a hidden, surprising way: not the restoration of an earthly kingdom to Israel, but the founding of a community of the Spirit, in a world-wide fellowship of faith. So many Jews turn away, perplexed and uncertain, holding onto the Torah—as is only right—and unable to accept the strange new doctrines of the Trinity and incarnation which emerged in the early Church. They still look for the Messiah, for the coming of God's Kingdom; they still keep the Law of God; they remain true to their own calling. So Christians and Jews alike await a common goal, the redemption of the world from evil by the glorious revelation of God's Chosen One. We who are not Jews, however, have been called into the sphere of God's friendship by the Spirit who brings the life of the crucified Christ into our hearts. We are a people chosen, not by birth, but by the preaching of the gospel of cross and resurrection.

Neither Jew nor Christian can give up their own proper calling. The Christian can and must confess that the Jewish tradition preserves much that is truly given by God: the Torah (the Law) and the Prophets. But he must remain true to his own belief that the Torah is fulfilled and transcended by the disclosure of the being of God in the person of Christ. However, he must also confess that the true glory of Christ will be manifest only at the end of history; and it may then be as far beyond his present very partial apprehension of Jesus as he thinks he is beyond the Old Testament Law. There is little reason to suppose that the Christian faith will continue to exist for ever in its present form. Looking back over two thousand years, we can see how much it has changed already; and how many more thousands of years have we to go? From being a Jewish sect which looked for the early return of the Messiah in glory, the Christian movement exploded throughout the Mediterranean world, coming to look more like a mystery-religion than anything else. It celebrated a dying and rising God; spoke of the divinization of man; revered the Queen of Heaven and encouraged ascetical mortification of the flesh. It fought against gnosticism and Neoplatonic paganism, but in the process it took on much of the character of its opponents.

Then, at the end of the Middle Ages, there was the rediscovery of Aristotle, by way of the Arabic commentators. That gave birth to a great new movement of systematization, which became Scholasticism, the rule of an intellectual Law over the minds of men. The Catholic Church attained the zenith of its power, as the only ark of salvation, teacher of the ultimate truth (by courtesy of Aristotle), a political and intellectual despotism, the only protection from barbarism. At the Reformation, the Church was divided, as Israel had been divided long ago. A new spirit of individualism arose, together with a strange new literalism of the written word, which tore authority away from one universal Church and handed it over to the translators and preachers who proclaimed the immediacy of each person's direct relationship to God, through a spiritual, but non-sacramental Christ. Now, at the present time, Christianity can be found in hundreds of forms. Its past conflicts with natural science and secularism have changed it for ever. So it is probably the most self-critical of all major faiths, still looking for reformulations of its ancient doctrines, which will meet our new understanding of the vastness of cosmic evolution.

C's book is an important sign of this search, challenging traditional beliefs as far as possible, in an attempt to get to the heart of the gospel, the growth in the life of the spirit. I appreciate how painful his quest is and how necessary it is to set out on it. I have written this book because I think he is wrong in his conclusions, but we can never return to the old formulations, the pre-critical forms of belief. Christian faith must go on growing and changing. At the basis of it all remains the claim that God was in Christ, reconciling the world to himself. My purpose in presenting this absurdly potted history of the Church has been to remind us of the different ways in which this claim has been seen. Each great change in our intellectual history requires a reformulation of the gospel. We only need to have a good sense of history, to see how Christian theology has changed completely in approach time and again, for us to accept that it must go on changing. God's revelation in Christ was not a complete presentation of truth, which puts a stop to all intellectual growth in religion or anywhere else. It was a revelation with all the mystery and infinite potential of a living person. It needs to be reapproached and reassessed in each new age. Its implicit richness will not be fully apparent until the whole of history has run its course.

All this moves us to look ahead to the fulness of the coming Christ. We cannot merely look back to ancient formulations in terms of unfamiliar philosophies. Nor can we deny the decisive act of God in Christ for our salvation. It is our vision of that act which must change, as our perspective is continually enlarged by a growing knowledge of our world. We cannot now predict what will emerge at last. But we would be most unwise to insist that present Christian institutions, practices and theologies have got it finally right. What I am suggesting is that increasing understanding of other forms of theistic belief may well help us to see some of the as yet hidden riches of Christ. In particular, until Jew and Christian are one, we will neither of us have a complete apprehension of the one who was rightly termed 'King of the Jews'. We may see ourselves, then, as moving towards a focus of unity, in the being of God. But, though our present understanding of Christ may change in ways we cannot foresee, we have to insist that Christ is the revelation of God and the redeemer of humanity. On that point, we cannot surrender our claim to have the truth, however much we confess our partial understanding of it.

In this respect, there does seem to be a basic conflict between Islam and this Christian belief. The ideas of incarnation and atonement seem to Muslims to be idolatrous and unnecessary. The whole existence of Islam is an insistence on the strictest monotheism, and on the finality of a written, unchangeable Word of God, the Koran. It may well be seen as a judgement on the European parochialism of much Christianity. There are possibilities of development in the very varied Muslim traditions. Critical study of the Koran, in a scholarly sense, has not yet begun in Muslim countries; and it is probably its pre-critical nature which accounts for its popularity in many parts of the world. It is simple and clear in outline, but such things as Sufism, though sceptically viewed by the orthodox, show the possibility of reinterpretation. Once again, we cannot pre-judge the future. Things will undoubtedly change and develop. But we cannot say how. Perhaps Christians will be able to develop a doctrine of incarnation more clearly guarded against the charge of idolatry, which Muslims bring against it, or a doctrine of the Trinity more unequivocally stressing the unity of God. Some would think this has been virtually done already. Perhaps Muslims will be able to adopt a less literalist attitude to their Scripture, and a less traditionalist social theology, while retaining their concern for justice and for the sovereignty of God. Whatever we may hope for, at the moment, we must remain committed to the truth as we see it now. So the Christian will want to testify to the personal love of God revealed in Christ; to the divine identification with creatures and redemption of the world, as well as to the austere transcendence of a God, who sternly warns and judges and whose inscrutable will is to be obeyed.

Judaism and Islam must appear to a Christian to be revelations of the being of God which find their correction and completion in Christ. But we may add that *our understanding* of Christ may itself need to be corrected by a better appreciation of what exists in other religious traditions, and by a less rigid insistence on the verbal formulae of past intellectuals, which happen to have become standard in some churches. We need a theology of other religions, if we are to see the revealing activity of God in its widest context. The attempt in this chapter is mainly meant to show that it is not good enough to give up our central beliefs, in order to get unity with others. It is truth which is important. We must seek truth in as wide a context as possible.

We may indeed find so much truth in a Buddhist tradition, and so little in certain traditional formulae of Christian tradition, that we may wish to call ourselves 'Buddhist Christians', or 'Christian Buddhists'. Why should we not do so, if it suits us? There is even a positive virtue in it, if it helps to release us from the terrible tendency to put everyone in a little box, with a package-deal of beliefs which they have to take on board wholesale. But there is a danger in it, too. We must not turn it into yet another little box, inside which sits what C calls 'the religious man of the future'. For he will have his check-list of beliefs, too; only, in his box, you only qualify as 'sound' if you cross enough beliefs off as false, instead of having to tick them as true.

The man in C's box is the man with spirituality but no doctrine. I have already argued (ch. 7) that such an alleged 'spirituality' is irrational, if it does not seek to relate appropriately to the nature of the world. The fact is, of course, that he does have a doctrine: a materialistic and atheistic doctrine, a doctrine as far removed from that of traditional Buddhism as it is from traditional

Christianity. That doctrine is just as disputed, as unverifiable and as speculative as the doctrine, which I believe to be true, that God exists, reveals himself and redeems the world in and through Jesus.

It is a very puzzling and mysterious fact that intelligent people disagree so much about such doctrines, but they do. I have tried to suggest that God reveals himself in some way and to some extent in every place which is not completely darkened by evil. And while the human responses to his revelation are always partial and inadequate, he has truly and fully shown himself in Jesus. This is not a sort of revelation which compels the assent of all who hear of it, or which is immune from misunderstanding. So we may wonder how we can be sure that this is the full revelation. From the human side, from the side of our believing, we have to say that we simply cannot regard all alleged revelations as equally partial or incomplete. Where claims conflict, we have to choose one. That is not arrogance; nor should it lead to intolerance. It is logically unavoidable, and compatible with the greatest respect for the different opinions of others. It is, quite simply, our opinion that it is true. But that does not mean it is just 'true for us' (a senseless phrase if ever there was one), as though something else could be true for other people. If it is true, it is true. Either God created the world or he did not. We cannot demonstrate its truth to everyone. But we believe it to be really true. There is no escape from the necessity of making such choices. So what matters is that we choose as sincerely as possible, with as wide a knowledge as possible, and with a certain self-critical awareness of what we are doing. So I believe that God has revealed himself fully in Jesus, because I sincerely think it is true. I know you may think otherwise; and so I think that you must stick to your sincere opinion, too.

It follows that I think that non-Christians are mistaken about the nature of God and of his redemption of the human race. It does not follow at all that they are not redeemed. If God is the sort of love that I believe the cross reveals, he will redeem all who do not, in the end, positively reject him. In other words, Christ redeems the world, even if most people have never heard of him. We do not have to have heard of him, to be redeemed by him; just as we do not need to know who saves us from a terrible flood; we can still be saved. Of course, redemption cannot be completed in this quite unconscious way. Since it consists in a personal union with God, and since Christ is the mediator of this union, the human form of God, no one can finally achieve redemption without conscious knowledge and love of Christ. After death, all will come to know by whom they have been saved; and they will only be saved as and when they come to know him as Lord and Saviour. But in this world, we cannot ever search the hearts of men, to know their innermost standing before God. All we can do is search our own hearts, and be sincere in our search for truth and for moral integrity.

This search has led me to think that the most coherent, comprehensive, consistent and intelligible account of the nature of the world is theism. It has led me to think that the highest sort of ideal is that presented by Jesus in his life and teaching: an ideal which only makes sense in the context of a world freely created by love and disfigured by human hatred, weakness and fear. It has led me to see that in this world our most fundamental and important beliefs are incapable of objective verification; in that sense, we are in a world without answers. In this world, Christianity does not come along, offering the answers. Christ comes, saying 'Follow me'. Some do and some do not; we cannot say why. Some who follow him become bitter or disillusioned; some use his name to gain power over others. Some, a few, find in him a deep, growing, transforming relationship to God, the personal reality of the world. Then faith blossoms, the gift of grace which gives hope in a hopeless world, forgiveness and charity in a world of harsh antagonisms. That faith shines in the world, like a light set on a hill, flickering but bright in the darkness. It is a hidden prefiguring of heaven, a parable open and concealed at once, a tree of crucifixion and eternal life. The darkness of a world, which has chosen against God, continues. If we are called to the light, it is not for our superior intellects nor for our moral excellence; nor are we to be chosen for happiness, while the others sail on to despair. We are called to serve, to witness, to live out the life of Christ, to fill out the number of his sufferings and to be his hands and feet as members of his body.

So the Christian life is a life held fast in objective uncertainty. It is a life of faith, lived out in paradox and mystery. It is lived out in response to a vision we see and lose and see again, but never grasp. Our little systems and petty ideas are built out of response to this vision. They are, as C puts it, 'works of human art and the vehicles of cherished spiritual values and intuitions' (166). When they are too neat, too cut-and-dried, too restrictive, we must drop them, but we cannot live without them, without new ones to take their place. My fundamental objection to C's proposed religion is that it is itself too Scholastic, too neat and tidy and too restrictive of human knowledge and possibilities. It is a thin, flavourless faith, with all the mystery squeezed out and drained away; and all because he does not like the old tyrant-god, ordering people about, tenuously clinging to existence at the edge of the scientific world-picture. Well, neither do I. Let us have, instead, a God who is perfectly realized Spirit, the personal heart of a vast cosmos directed to evolving embodied and responsive finite spirits which can share in his inexhaustible life. We may look for signs and sacraments of that ultimate reality in the world around us, and particularly in the great focal-points of traditions of prayer, Gautama, Moses, Jesus, Mohammed, Krishna. We may find his personal reality enshrined and expressed in Jesus, the longed-for Messiah of Israel. We may seek to see his self-giving love spreading throughout the world from that point, to redeem it from self-will and bring it to fulfilment by creative co-operation with him. This particular way of expressing the Christian vision has only been possible since the rise of modern science, with its evolutionary vision and its renewed emphasis on time and history. It is a vision for today, responding in its own way to the divine mystery which is in Christ. It is not a vision which takes leave of God. On the contrary, it holds fast to God, as the dynamic and creative source of our responsive faith, the objective reality which we find mediated through focal embodiments in our world and which inspires our changing, developing attempts to understand and articulate it in symbols and concepts. It is that God himself, in his existent reality, who is the ultimate goal of the religious life, the source of the intelligibility of the world, the realization of our moral ideals and the guarantor that finally 'all will be well, and all manner of things will be well'. We may take leave of an image of God, but God himself will never let us go.